The First Australians

The First Australians

BY RONALD M. BERNDT AND

CATHERINE H. BERNDT

URE SMITH . SYDNEY

Third edition (hardcover, revised and enlarged)
published in 1974 by
Ure Smith, Sydney
176 South Creek Road, Dee Why West, NSW 2099
a division of IPC Books Pty Limited

First published in Australia (hardcover edition)
in 1952 by
Ure Smith Pty Ltd
Second edition (hardcover) 1967

Preface

Let us introduce you to an Australian minority — the Aborigines, the First Australians, who, before the coming of Europeans, occupied the whole of this Continent and its immediate islands . . .

Under the full impact of the new order, they rapidly dwindled away about the settled areas. Farther inland they were for a time protected: but, as settlers and explorers spread over much of the Continent, the same tale was repeated. At the same time the life they knew, into which they had been born, became in many places altered beyond recognition.

In the following pages we try to show you something of the way in which these people lived, what it was that gave their lives meaning and colour. Remember, this is only an outline. Details vary from one tribe to another: but on broad general lines the pattern we have traced is not obscured by a mass of material, however vital and interesting it may be. For the reader anxious to pursue the subject further, various publications are listed at the end of this volume.

Let us try to understand and appreciate these First Australians — people who were so admirably adjusted to the environment with which we now, at times, find ourselves in conflict: whose cultures were, and in some places still are, vivid living realities, splashed with brilliant colouring, virile, meaningful: people possessed of a religious zeal and a faith in life, a faith in the essential goodness and significance of their own way — the Aboriginal Way. But this Way was so patterned that its possessors found it hard to combat the alien invader; and it was based on premises contrary to those of the European — a different Way, involving different criteria and values. It had simply developed along different lines from ours — different in kind, not in quality nor in degree. Moreover it was, and is, contemporary: not an ancient survival, arrested in development, nor radically confined through mental retardation.

It is this point which we are apt to forget, as our Western European culture, with its complex organization and its stress on technology and wealth, spreads across the face of the earth, laying waste or absorbing other ideologies and patterns of life. We are apt to forget, too, that other peoples have developed through the centuries, adjusting themselves to their peculiar environment, evolving their own answers to the problems of existence, and finding in them satisfaction and meaning within the framework of human reference.

Through trying to understand the behaviour of others, such as the Australian Aborigines, we come closer to understanding ourselves. Here is a way of life built up by one group of people: what value have they found in it, what satisfaction, what happiness?

And although the Aborigines are people physically different from us, who possess a culture dissimilar to our own, yet with all that they are human beings with the same basic urges, desires, and requirements as ourselves . . .

•   •   •

These words introduced the first edition of this book, more than twenty years ago. What we said then is still relevant and bears repeating — except that perhaps it is not necessary, now, to labour the point made in the last paragraph. In re-issuing the volume, the publishers wanted to retain the main text intact, but to replace most of the original black and white illustrations with coloured ones and to telescope the three earlier prefaces. Chapter XXI was added in 1966. We would have liked to alter the text, at least to modify the style here and there. But the outcome would have been a more substantial work, very different from its original intent. A fuller account — a more detailed outline, so to speak — is available in *The World of the First Australians.*

In recent years, against a background of increasing political awareness, people of Aboriginal descent have become more vocal, mostly on the subjects of Aboriginal welfare and Aboriginal rights. In one sense, and without minimizing the importance of international pressures, their demands were triggered off by the dramatic increase in exploitation of mineral and other resources, particularly in the Northern Territory, but also in Queensland and in Western and South Australia. But that was barely an issue when we first wrote this book. And public interest in it, and in other matters affecting Aborigines, was slight and sporadic — almost negligible, in proportion to the problems that were building up, unnoticed by the majority of Australians.

Only a few decades ago, anyone who showed concern for Aboriginal welfare was likely to be dismissed as a crank or a Communist, or worse. The safest and most usual attitude was one of indifference with an overlay of tolerance, a kind of middle ground between abstract benevolence and patronizing contempt. Today, as before, feelings of resentment or superiority or both can lie behind a helping hand or a militant zeal for Aboriginal Rights. Prejudice or outright hostility are not hard to find, and even openly admitted — especially as a 'backlash' response, or among immigrants who see 'blacks' (variously defined) as a threat or a nuisance. But statements of this sort are likely to be pounced on by Aboriginal welfare associations and by student groups, because the emphasis now, publicly at least, is all in the other direction.

This point, however, has not been reached without

a long series of struggles, most of them unreported by the news media of their day and virtually unrecorded. Police documents and others, particularly on the early days of contact but also on later events, note some and hint at many more. Nearly all such events (clashes, conflicts, confrontations) were small in scale and locally centred. Organized protests really began during the 1940's, and attention from the press and other media stimulated as well as reflected the changing national approach. Two pertinent examples in the late 1960's were the Guirindji Case and the Gove Land Rights Dispute.

In the first, Aborigines at Wave Hill pastoral station went on strike for better wages, housing and employment conditions. They also wanted a stretch of Guirindji tribal land (or what *had* been Guirindji tribal land) restored to them for their own use and control, and this aspect assumed greater magnitude as the strike proceeded. Late in 1972, they were granted a leasehold (not freehold) of land excised from Wave Hill.

The second case, more far-reaching in its implications, centred primarily on a huge bauxite project on the Gove Peninsula in north-eastern Arnhem Land, in what was officially an Aboriginal Reserve. Local Aborigines sued the Nabalco Mining Company *and* the Commonwealth of Australia on several fronts, seeking compensation and/or an injunction to restrain mining activities, and recognition of their land rights. The case had wide publicity, but the outcome was the judgement that neither they nor any other Aborigines had any legal claim to or in the land on the basis of their traditional occupancy of it — on the grounds that all previous claims had been superseded by the taking-over of the entire continent for the British crown.

Two social anthropologists had agreed to support the Aborigines' claims by preparing written evidence and also appearing in court. (Professor W. E. H. Stanner focused on the general question of Aboriginal relations with the land. R. M. Berndt concentrated on the position in Arnhem Land, with specific reference to the disputed region — the north-eastern corner centring on Gove and Yirrkalla.) This illustrates very well the dual concern of social anthropologists involved in the Aboriginal field: one side emphasizing academic and theoretical issues, the other underlining the necessary linkage between research and practical welfare. Professor A. P. Elkin himself displayed this sense of social responsibility over a long period, and encouraged it in others. But up to the early 1950's there were, in fact, very few others: social-cultural anthropologists were scarce in Australia, and those attracted to Aboriginal research were scarcer still. The same thing applied to physical anthropology, linguistics and archaeology. Most such research was carried out by university departments and museums. The establishment of the Australian Institute of Aboriginal Studies, in 1961, gave a tremendous impetus to all of it. This Institute symbolizes an upsurge of interest in the First Australians — an interest which, somewhat ironically, coincides with the continuing disappearance of their traditional way of life. After 1967, the Federal Council (Office) of Aboriginal Affairs, among its varying activities, has also supported research — especially where it seems directly relevant to problem-solving.

Nevertheless, what could be called uniquely Aboriginal is becoming much less so. Even in regions like Arnhem Land and the Central and

Western Deserts, where the quality of life still has a traditional flavour, the contrast is simply relative: the patterns of living are less European than elsewhere, but less 'Aboriginal' than they were in the immediate past.

In the light of this situation, we might well ask — all of us, including Aboriginal Australians — whether traditional Aboriginal society and culture have any relevance to contemporary living. There are several answers, but three immediate ones come to mind. First, a great deal of traditional life does survive, in one form or another. Secondly, because this exists and is increasingly vulnerable to change, it has a direct bearing on the consideration of practical welfare problems. Thirdly, and perhaps the most vital, it represents an Aboriginal heritage and a social identity for all persons of Aboriginal descent[1].

The history of Aboriginal-European contact over the years has taught us not to underestimate the significance of economic factors. But an emotional basis for living is almost equally important. Current protest and Black Power manifestations in this country do not only take up specific matters such as land rights, discrimination and prejudice. In a more general sense, they react against real or supposed European domination and direction and the lack of opportunity for people of Aboriginal descent to participate effectively in decisions affecting the course of their lives. But basically, behind all of this is a search for a special niche in the Australian scene. And that special place, many of them recognize, can be had only through emphasizing their Aboriginal background. Over and above the legitimate role of academic research, then, the Australian Institute of Aboriginal Studies, the Federal Office of Aboriginal

Affairs, and the Advisory Committee on Aboriginal Arts (Australian Council for the Arts) are all concerned, each in its own way, in sustaining an interest in that traditional heritage, or in some form of it — even though it will no longer be set within its living matrix.

Aborigines made this Continent their own, and because of their especially intimate association with their natural environment, their place in its history is beyond dispute; the life they led here cannot be altogether irrelevant to the people who followed them or intermixed with them. It is a vital part of the Australian heritage. Indirectly, it concerns the Australian nation as a whole. Directly, and specifically, it is the heritage of those Australians who are wholly or partly Aboriginal in descent. The fact that many of them actually know little or nothing of it except at second-hand does not make it less significant to them.

The picture that is emerging for literate people of Aboriginal descent is a composite one, not tied to any particular region but of a kind that could be called 'generalized Aboriginal'. And a large part of it, although certainly not all, will be derived (as some of it is now, in long-settled areas) from written sources, rather than from what they themselves have learnt through first-hand experience. Current programmes designed to 'teach Aboriginal culture' to Aboriginal school-children will reinforce this trend.

In realistic terms, the future of all Aborigines is linked inevitably with other Australians in the wider society. This is particularly true both economically and educationally. It is also true in so far as traditional life is concerned. The Aborigines were a non-literate people, with no durable records of their own affairs: all knowledge was handed on by word of mouth. So, virtually all of the written material relating to them derives from the efforts and initiative of others — a fact that not all of them appreciate. Those people of Aboriginal descent who have become literate and sufficiently skilled to take this step themselves have already been estranged, in varying degrees, from traditional Aboriginal culture. When they turn their attention to this aspect of their own background, they will be coming to it almost as strangers — or, if they have been trained anthropologically, as anthropologists, and not as functional members of a living traditional Aboriginal society. Of course, persons like Ken Colbung, Jack Davis, Lazarus Lamilami, Charles Perkins, Phillip Roberts, Dick Roughsey, and Kath Walker, and others have contributed immeasurably to a personal view of Aboriginality. But they have done so from a perspective which is actually, in differing degrees, far removed from that traditional life.

Australians, Aboriginal and otherwise, saw the 1967 Referendum[2] as a turning point in the sad story of Aboriginal-European relations — not because of the Census question, but because they saw Federal intervention as opening up a fresh and entirely different chapter. Things did not work out exactly as they hoped. Perhaps they expected too much, too quickly, in a field crowded with a long accumulation of obstacles. Actually, new developments were taking place and others were foreshadowed: the Office of Aboriginal Affairs, increased funds, and guidance and stimulation for projects ranging over a wide spectrum. These did not still the rising complaints of 'too slow' and 'not enough', and grumbling about a variety of matters:

health, employment, housing, education and, not least, land rights. Numbers of small protests crystallized in the Canberra Tent affair.

On the lawns outside Parliament House in Canberra on Australia Day, January 26th, 1972, a group of people of Aboriginal descent and their supporters set up a camp which they designated an Embassy, drawing national and international attention to the subject of Aboriginal Land Rights. Apart from tourist interest, however, what attracted attention was not so much the tents themselves as the events in July 1972 when 'Embassy' members defied an order to remove them. The dramatic scenes of violence and confusion, as Commonwealth police moved in to demolish the tents and arrest their defenders, provided strong television meat for viewers at home and abroad. A second demolition in September 1972 met only passive resistance, and similar 'embassies' in South and Western Australia ran their course peacefully without police intervention. Of course, both of these States had Labor governments, and it was hard to escape the conclusion that they were interested in showing the Federal government just how such matters should be handled.

This was a Federal election year. As polling time (December 1972) approached, Aboriginal welfare emerged as a salient issue and, to an unprecedented degree, an arena of competition between the main political parties. Increased funds, in promise or actuality, and a greater readiness to listen to Aboriginal views and opinions, were features of the day. The Labor Party's victory at the polls was followed, early in 1973, by moves to set in train a series of new reforms, or to accelerate reforms instituted by its predecessor. The new Minister for Aboriginal Affairs already had a reputation for an aggressive concern with Aboriginal welfare. One of his first official statements insisted that the notoriously high infant mortality rate among people of Aboriginal descent would be effectively reduced — or (as press reports put it) 'heads would roll'. A well-known legal practitioner was appointed to look into the whole question of Aboriginal land rights. And there is a growing awareness among mining companies themselves of the need to consider traditional and religious sites on land earmarked for such 'development'; for instance, moves were begun in 1972 to set up a specialist committee to consider, not only this, but all aspects of Aborigines *vis-à-vis* mining.

Here, in short, is another turning point: but this time, the changes are already accelerating. And for a great many Australians, if not all, the mood is one of cautious optimism.

In this book our aim has been to show something of the Aboriginal side of the Australian heritage, in the hope that readers will be stimulated to explore it further. It is not designed for specialists but as an introduction to a subject on which *all* Australians should not merely have opinions: they should be reasonably well-informed, too — a subject which no one who wants to know about Australia can afford to neglect.

RONALD M. BERNDT
CATHERINE H. BERNDT
Department of Anthropology,
University of Western Australia.
1973.

(xiv)

Contents

I	Perspective	19
II	Physical and Cultural Diversity	27
III	The Tribes	34
IV	Making a Living	39
V	Trade	46
VI	Growing Up	49
VII	The Cycle of Life	56
VIII	Men and Women	58
IX	The Meaning of Life	65
X	Symbolism in Religion	71
XI	Mythology	76
XII	Ritual and Ceremony	84
XIII	Songs	92
XIV	Artist and Craftsman	95
XV	Law and Order	101
XVI	Behaving	105
XVII	Magic and Sorcery	111
XVIII	Death and What Follows	115
XIX	Values	119
XX	The Changing World	123
XXI	The Future	128
	Notes	141
	References	147

Illustrations

Full Descriptions Appear Against Each Plate

Plates

1 to 10	Camp scenes	Colour	24
11 to 14	Children	Colour	32
15 & 16	Children	Colour	48
17 to 23	Desert life: water, food and equipment I	Colour	48
24 to 27	Desert life: water, food and equipment I	Colour	64
28 to 30	Desert life: water, food and equipment II	Black & white	64
31 to 38	Desert life: water, food and equipment II	Black & white	72
39 to 42	Desert life: water, food and equipment II	Black & white	80
43 & 44	Cave paintings	Colour	80
45 to 48	Cave paintings	Colour	88
49 to 51	Cave paintings	Colour	96
52 to 54	Artists at work	Colour	96
55	Artists at work	Colour	104
56 to 62	An Arnhem Land circumcision ritual	Colour	104
63 to 67	The Elcho Island Memorial; a Morning Star emblem; mortuary dancing; a didjeridu player and songman	Colour	112
68 to 70	Mortuary dancing, Arnhem Land	Colour	112
71 to 74	Mortuary dancing, Arnhem Land	Colour	120
75 to 80	Mortuary ritual, Melville and Bathurst Islands	Colour	120
81 to 85	Mortuary ritual, Melville and Bathurst Islands	Colour	128

(xvi)

The day breaks—the first rays of the rising Sun,
stretching her arms.
Daylight breaking, as the Sun rises to her feet.
Sun rising, scattering the darkness;
lighting up the land . . .
With disc shining, bringing daylight,
as the birds whistle and call . . .
People are moving about, talking, feeling the warmth.
Burning through the Gorge, she rises,
walking westwards,
Wearing her waist-band of human hair.
She shines on the blossoming coolibah tree,
with its sprawling roots,
Its shady branches spreading . . .

(Fragment from the sacred Dulngulg cycle—Mudbara tribe, Wave Hill, Northern Territory. The Sun rises warming the land.)

AUSTRALIA

SHOWING SOME OF THE MAIN
PLACES MENTIONED IN THIS BOOK

CHAPTER I

Perspective

WE Australians who live in the cities about our Southern coastlines see and know, for the most part, nothing but what we call the European way of life —a way of life uprooted and transplanted by succeeding generations of migrants to an alien land. To them as to us it was a new country, with unlimited potentialities, to which we brought our cultural patterns, our modes of behaviour, our form of social organization. Thus within the span of less than two centuries we have transformed the face of a country with our own particular brand of civilization.

Almost completely swept from our towns and cities is any trace of the people who once proudly roamed our land. Only within the walls of museums are relics recalling their past existence: lifeless skeletal material, which tells us little or nothing of the people themselves.

Away from the cities and towns, we may travel for hundreds of miles before discovering evidence that these First Australians ever really inhabited this vast land. The

19

kitchen midden, the old camp site, the rock carving or painting, the marked tree, the scattered flint, are discernible only after search, and significant only to the initiated few.

Nevertheless, as our gaze sharpens and our interest deepens we can find further indications that people of other than Austro-European stock once inhabited the country we now call Australia. Still in our towns and cities are mixed bloods and even occasionally full bloods, usually a minority to all intents and purposes inarticulate.³ Some of them have become more or less assimilated with us. Others remain dispossessed, living out their lives on Government and Mission stations, having lost most, if not all, of the traditional background which belonged to their forebears.

As we move further away from close European settlement, signs of their presence become more apparent. More Government and Mission stations make their appearance, and these different people are gathered in greater numbers. We find them working around small country towns, or on sheep and cattle stations. And in some places, parts of central Australia or along the northern coasts, they still wander across their tribal territories, hunting and collecting, living the life they appreciate and love—the life which is the Aboriginal Way.

Transplanted from our cities, from our towns, into the real Australian environment, among these Aborigines we are perplexed—strangers in what we consider our own land. We are familiar with the bush, its trees and shrubs, animals and birds: these are things of which we have some knowledge, some means of classifying on the basis of our own experience. Once the initial reaction has subsided, we can readily feel at home in the acacia and spinifex bush of the Great Victoria Desert, the corrugated sand dunes of the Centre, the rocky low-lying hills around Ernabella and Hermannsburg—the Musgraves and Macdonnells, with their changing hues, their rugged beauty: the grassy plains adjacent to inland rivers, the monotonous coastline with its gaps of curving beach and mangrove swamps, its low-lying islands: and inland again to billabongs edged with pandanus, covered with lilies: or mile upon mile of bush, blackened by sweeping fires, springing to greenery after recent rains. Changing scenery, changing climate: from arid wastes of sand and stone and stunted growth, to fertile lands abounding in all sorts of natural game, with plants, bushes and trees growing in lively profusion: now dry heat, now moist humidity, or biting cold. There is nothing strange here, only variations of what we already know.

But within this environment which we call typically Australian are other human beings, less familiar to most of us, less easily catalogued and pigeon-holed into our frame of reference, or correlated with our own experience. Human beings, moreover, dark in skin colour, who wear little or no clothing, carry simple weapons, behave in a fashion that does not conform to our recognized and established patterns, speak languages that we do not understand, dance and sing in ways that our untuned ears and untrained eyes find exotic, barbaric and even primitive. Men, women and children moving from camp to camp, hunting and food-collecting: thinking, acting, living in ways that seem strange to us.

Who are these people? What do they really think? How do they really live? These are some of the many questions we must ask ourselves when we come into contact with them for the first time—questions which must remain unanswered unless we break down the barrier of language, live with them and come to appreciate their outlook on life. Few of us can really hope to do this. Learning

21

a language takes time and effort. Living with them, becoming adjusted to their ways and sublimating our own, requires more time, as well as training and experience. In a superficial way we can learn a lot by observation, by living in outback localities where these Aborigines⁴wander, by employing them for odd jobs, and so on. Or if we are missionaries or Government administrators we may perhaps accumulate something more than a superficial knowledge; but then our very presence as representatives of an alien form of Government, or as teachers, prevents us from entering very deeply into their traditional life.

To a large extent we must rely on the trained anthropologist to accomplish a task that at first glance appears almost impossible. He, or she, spends a great deal of his time living with groups like these, trying to understand them, to learn their languages or dialects, so that through his efforts the unfamiliar may become familiar, and the unknown, known.

Through his eyes the things we see attain meaning, and the haze of strangeness evaporates, to be replaced by clearer perception, greater understanding, and comprehension of the ways and thoughts of these Aborigines. We see them not as exotic primitives, strange survivals with a stone-age culture, but as contemporaries, modern men and women, motivated by the same basic urges as ourselves, but with a different way of life, a different outlook, different values—one of the many variations on the theme of human beings.

These people are the real—the First—Australians, who possessed this land of ours long before the visits of early explorers. They lived here for countless centuries undisturbed, in comparative isolation. Their way of life was a Way that had been developed over many generations, modified and amplified to suit them as time went by.

Against a common background, they showed many variations from one area to another: but none of them remained wholly static. People of different groups came into contact, and between neighbouring tribes there was gradual but steady interchange of ideas and techniques. Yet within the common Aboriginal framework they were restricted, bound by certain environmental limitations. Lacking constant stimulation from outside sources, and influenced by their particular personalities and psychological outlook, their pattern of living developed inevitably along more or less specialized lines.

The Aborigines were intimately acquainted with their environment, knowing personally the land, and all its natural species, and the regularly changing seasons. Within their social limitations their life was full, and they obtained virtually all they desired. They grew, loved and died believing themselves to be part of a comprehensible and universal scheme arranged primarily for their benefit. There was no real strangeness, no grappling with essentially unknown elements, nor unforeseen conditions. They were sure of themselves, and of the culture in which they had grown; they could cope with all they met, all they saw and all they heard. There was no real struggle for survival, even in the most arid regions, of the kind that we ourselves know in our own mechanized and highly complex culture; no extreme poverty, nor monopolization.

With the coming of the European—the alien—the delicate balance of their life was sharply upset.

In the fertile southern coastal regions the Aborigines felt the full blow of the stranger's presence. They were conservative, unprepared for the great changes which were upon them, unable to deal with the new problems that confronted them. Much of what they encountered seemed to them inexplicable, and even alarming: a

23

strange language, and strange customs based on different values. Worse still, they were dispossessed of lands which they had looked upon as irrevocably theirs, lands that were associated spiritually with themselves and their tribal ancestors. When they tried to defend what they considered their rights, they were shot and driven back: even when they did not retaliate they were shot and hunted, their women-folk debauched and abducted.

As the European settlers gradually spread inland, the same story marked their progress: until eventually, as the years passed, only remnants were left around the towns and cities, about the homesteads and cattle stations. Others gathered on specially formed settlements, protected artificially from the devastatingly rapid effects of this alien impact. But their traditional life had been radically disturbed. Because they could no longer roam at will over their own lands—their heritage—and because many of them were dead, or collected in supervised camps, the life they knew came to an end as a living reality. Much remained, and continues to remain, but the delicate mainspring of their culture was broken.

In outlying regions, where European settlement is sparse, reluctant, or even forbidden—parts of the inland, the Centre, the northern coasts—the Aborigine may still live a life approximating that which his ancestors found so congenial. Approximating, no more: for today in the whole of Australia there is no uncontacted Aboriginal group: no tribe or horde which has not had some association, at least indirect, with the alien intruders: no single Aborigine who has not heard of the white man.

Nevertheless, there are still groups of Aborigines who continue to live almost in their traditional way, with only spasmodic contact with Europeans. Their number is steadily growing smaller, as more and more of them come to spend most of their time on some Mission

1. Camp scene, Central Australia. Men resting by a windbreak; one uses a spearthrower as an adze.
Photograph : courtesy C. P. Mountford

2. Family group sheltered by a windbreak. Gibson Desert area, 1965.
Photograph : courtesy I. Dunlop

3. Quasi-traditional desert camp. Ernabella area, northern South Australia, 1967.
Photograph: courtesy N. M. Wallace

4. Quasi-traditional arrangement of shelters made of boughs and blankets. Balgo Hills, Western Australia, 1960.

5. People relaxing beside their shelters. Balgo Hills, 1960.

6. Stringybark wet-season or mosquito huts. Buckingham Bay, north-eastern Arnhem Land, 1961.

7. Huts and shelters by the sea. Elcho Island, north-eastern Arnhem Land, 1964. The shelters are traditional in style, the huts of European origin.

8. Beach-camp scene. Yirrkalla, north-eastern Arnhem Land, 1964.

9. Boiling tea. Goulburn Island, western Arnhem Land, 1961.

10. Traditional shelters, Melville Island, 1954.
Photograph : courtesy C. P. Mountford

station or Government settlement. And so their traditional life recedes, until it becomes superseded by new ways; and finally the time comes when they know nothing of the life of their forefathers.

This is no unique manifestation. It is common the world over, and has not been confined to any particular age or period in the history of mankind.

But because such cultural impacts and changing ideologies are so frequently found, this does not excuse us from trying to understand what is happening—however inevitable the process may seem. No one person nor Government body can control it, for it must always follow more or less close contact between two groups with widely differing values. True, the impact can be cushioned, conditioned in such a way that its full force is not felt at once, but is diffused gradually over a period. Then the people involved can make their own adjustments to the changing times, influenced as they must be by the dominant group.

And so, as we move out from our cities and towns; as we go further inland, leaving behind us the well-made roads, the brilliant lights, the noise and teeming multitudes of our own kind, we eventually find these people, the Aborigines—the First Australians. The dispossessed, whose prototypes once wandered across every part of this Continent of ours; who divided up fertile and arid country alike into tribal territories; who named every hill, river, plain and bay, and linked them with a vivid mythology; who knew the natural products of this land, for on that knowledge depended their livelihood; who possessed a faith in the environment and in the life they knew.

And knowing of their existence, some of us desire to know more. What manner of people were these First Australians who once roamed the land on which our

25

cities and towns have risen, where our homes are built, and where our way of life is supreme?

Laintjung, Ancestral Being; a wooden carving from Yirr-kalla, eastern Arnhem Land.

CHAPTER 11

Physical and Cultural Diversity

NOBODY knows just how long the Australian Aborigines have lived on this Continent, nor whence they originally came. Theories there are in plenty. Some postulate India, others Indonesia, as their original 'home', or suggest that they crossed over the land 'bridge' separating New Guinea from Cape York—and so on. But their origin is shrouded in antiquity, and speculation is fruitless.[5]

Except for the Tasmanoids, and a couple of like 'pockets' now virtually extinct, they represent some conformity of physical type, but much diversity in head-shape and stature. Although we are not considering them from the standpoint of the physical anthropologist, we must remember these physical variations, for quite probably they are linked with variations in culture.

The social anthropologist who has worked with a cross-section of these Aborigines, moving from one place to another, has his own impressions to offer. He may have noticed the extreme hairiness of the tribal groups

27

about the Lower River Murray and lakes district in South Australia, where some men had chest and body hair nine inches or so long, some women beards and moustaches. Then in the Great Victoria Desert, stretching northwards from the East-West (Transcontinental) Railway Line to the central ranges of the Everards, Musgraves, Tomlinsons, Petermans and Warburtons, the people have copper-coloured skin, sloping foreheads, prominent brow-ridges, with almost aquiline noses; most of them are slightly built, with muscular bodies and thin shanks, few of them tall. In Central Australia are people sometimes described as 'typically' Aboriginal, with even more distinct brow-ridges, deep-set eyes and broad nostrils. Some of their women folk, like those of the Tanami-Granites 'desert' north-westwards to Halls' Creek, down towards the Canning Stock route, and even near Lilla Creek in northern South Australia, have fair copper-tinted hair. Towards the borders of the Northern Territory and Western Australia, in this 'desert' country, are people with Jewish-like profiles and prominent noses —short men and women, thin and wiry from constant movement in search of food. Further north again, towards the coast, the Aborigines are bigger-boned, taller and heavier. Some are almost European in appearance, except for their chocolate brown pigmentation and dark brown eyes, while others again have the typically Centralian features of wide nostrils, strong brow-ridge, thick jowls, or receding forehead and chin. On Melville and Bathurst Islands are people darker in colour, many of them heavily built, deep-chested and muscular. A few of the old men still wear their clipped tufty beards, fringing the face from ear to ear, unlike any found on the mainland.

In western Arnhem Land, too, are a number of short people, no more than four and a half to five feet high, from the source of the Liverpool River: some are small-boned, delicately shaped, a few thick set and squat. Along the northern Arnhem Land coast the physical range extends from the conventional Centralian type to lighter skinned people reminiscent of Indonesians. There are finely chiselled profiles, straight short noses, broad cheeks, inconspicuous brow-ridges, and lank straight hair: lips are thin, when contrasted with the full lips of the more inland groups, and bodies and legs well-developed, against the thin shanks of the desert hunters.

Nor is there conformity in the matter of hair texture, for some have coarse hair, while others have soft, fine, strands. Most Aborigines have wavy hair, some curly; and some of the women are proud of the reddish lights which need no red ochre to enhance them.

Thus there is not just one 'Aboriginal type', any more than there is an Australian or European type, but merely numbers of variations within a given range.

Just as there are physical differences, so there is and has been cultural diversity. While all over the Continent their way of life could be described as characteristically Aboriginal, it has been highlighted and enriched by hundreds of local manifestations.

All the Aborigines had certain features in common. They were semi-nomadic hunters and collectors, wandering across the land or fishing for their food, never living in settled villages, nor placing much stress on material possessions. Ordinarily, they were satisfied with the minimum of essentials. Most wore little or no clothing, and all had what we may loosely term the totemic view of nature. Living close to their natural environment, they saw themselves, the universe, and nature as inter-related parts of one whole, all functioning in unison, all inter-dependent.

Here, however, the similarity ends. There is no *lingua*

29

franca, no language by means of which a man could make himself understood from one end of the Continent to the other. Throughout Aboriginal Australia hundreds of languages were spoken, some of them made up of numerous dialects. People of one tribe[6] might be unfamiliar with the language spoken only a few miles away, while even when one language covered a wide area (as among the Wulamba bloc of north-eastern Arnhem Land) everyone needed to speak and understand at least two or three dialects.

On the whole, the tribes kept to themselves, meeting those speaking different languages only on ceremonial occasions, or perhaps when permission was granted to strangers to hunt through adjacent territory. Although this gives the appearance of tribal isolation, with clear-cut linguistic barriers, such was not always the case (as we shall see later on).

Hand in hand with this diversity of language, distinguishing one tribal group from another, went different patterns of living, each with its peculiar emphasis.

Some societies reckoned descent primarily through the mother, some through the father, while others attached almost equal importance to both. Rules governing marriage varied from region to region, from tribe to tribe; in one the most favoured mate was a cross-cousin, the daughter of one's mother's brother or father's sister, in another her daughter was the most desirable wife— and so on. Each society had its kinship structure, defining a person's relationship not only to blood and affinal kin, but indeed to each member of the tribe.

Environmental differences throughout the Continent have led to differences in economic approach, although these may be found even within the same area. There are coastal people, and folk of the inland rivers or fertile jungles; people living among the hills and rocks and

thick scrub of the inland, or wandering across comparatively arid wastes, with only occasional waterholes and
grassy plains. The way in which they have been forced to
obtain their daily sustenance has affected their whole
economy—not only the process of food-collecting and
hunting, but indeed the whole life of the tribe: for it
involves special techniques, special ways of living.

Religious experience with its substantiating mythology
varies, too, from one area to another. In some cases a
common thread may run from tribe to tribe over a wide
stretch of country, with its outward manifestations
broadly the same or strikingly different. Individual
features of song, music and dance may be widely diffused,
but during the process may change in function and
meaning. The sacred *djamalag* ritual of the great Fertility
cult, from the central west of the Northern Territory, is
in western Arnhem Land simply a trade dance with erotic
significance. Or women's secret religious ceremonies,
spreading across the Continent, become associated only
with love magic. In one area the *wonigi* emblems of
string or human hair twine are sacred, used only in the
most important religious rituals: in another, they figure
in 'playabout' ceremonies held in the main camp.

We can see, then, that what is true for one Aboriginal
group does not necessarily hold good for another. There
are weapons and utensils, for instance, found only in
one tribe: differing techniques for making and decorating
spears and spearthrowers, clubs, dilly-bags, and digging-
sticks. Boomerangs may be used in one community as
hunting weapons, in another as clapping sticks to beat
rhythmically in time to the singing; and in others they
are unknown, or not used at all.

Diversity in language not only helps to create different
ways of living, behaving, and thinking: over the years,
also, it reinforces and consolidates them; and knowledge

31

of one Aboriginal group (say, in eastern Arnhem Land) does not necessarily mean that we can speak with authority about others—people living in the Great Victoria Desert, or the 'rain forests' near Cairns, or the barren country about the Canning Stock route.

Aborigines from different regions, different tribes, will not react in exactly the same way to a given situation: for each responds in the light of his own upbringing and background—his traditional heritage, the unique pattern of life developed over countless centuries. Even within one tribe, no two personalities are exactly alike: everyone has his individual peculiarities, moulded and shaped by his own personal experience.

We must bear these points in mind: they are vital in helping us to understand the Aborigines, with all the rich variety of their life throughout the Continent.

Nevertheless, when contrasted with other peoples of the world, they show a basic similarity which links them together as essentially one. The differences between them recede in importance, as compared with those which mark them off from the alien invader—the European. Here there is sharp distinction, not only in physical appearance, but also in outlook and tradition.

The First Australian, faced with the European conqueror, was bewildered. There was no linguistic medium, no common points which he could grasp quickly to turn the situation to his advantage. And the newcomer, in his turn, found little among them which was congenial. To him they were part of the indigenous environment—people worlds apart from himself, wandering naked across the land for sustenance, always on the move, building no permanent homes but only flimsy shelters and wind-breaks: people with primitive weapons, and few material objects.

Because of this background, a product of their close

11. Playing in the Yirrkalla stream, 1964.

12. Searching for lice. Gibson Desert area, 1967.
Photograph : courtesy I. Dunlop

13. Helping to cut up a kangaroo: the boy's father uses a steel axe. Gibson Desert, 1965.
Photograph: courtesy I. Dunlop

14. Chewing *witjinti*, corkwood flowers which contain nectar. Kulpitjata, north-western South Australia, 1968.
Photograph: courtesy N. M. Wallace

bond with their environment, built up over years of comparative isolation, and because of the gulf which separated them from the Europeans—the newcomers—there was from the very beginning no doubt as to which of the two groups should dominate the other. Tribes with differing languages and emphases, with no sense of common nationality, could not combine as a war-making unit to drive out the invader. Even had this been possible, they had none of the material goods, the weapons, the political organization, without which they could not hope to succeed.

X-ray of a barramundi fish; from Oenpelli cave painting.

CHAPTER III

The Tribes

WHAT, then, is a tribe in Aboriginal Australia? A group of people related by actual or implied genealogy, speaking a common language, occupying a recognized tract of country over which they hunt and gather their food.

Sometimes the boundaries between one tribe and another are clearly defined, following natural features like rivers and hills. But often their territories overlap. Members of one tribe may have hunting rights over the country of another, or 'own' certain totemic sites there—and so on.

In size these tribal lands vary considerably, according to their fertility. Some of the largest are found in the 'deserts' of the Centre, where the Aborigines must hunt over large areas in which living is hard, and water is precious. But where food is plentiful people need not travel so far afield, and their tribal territories are smaller. The rich coastal lands, abounding in fish, can carry a greater density of population than the harsh Central plains, or the sandstone escarpments of the Arnhem Land interior. Small family groups need not move constantly over hundreds of miles in their battle for survival: but the tribes can cluster more closely together, with easier access to one another for fighting or trade. The Aranda (Arunta) of central Australia were much more widely scattered than the tribes along the Coorong and about the mouth of the River Murray, on the Daly River or along the Arnhem Land coast.

Mythology tells us much about tribal boundaries: for the Ancestral Beings, the Creative Spirits associated with local religion, are usually held responsible for all the most prominent natural features, and many of these have become totemic or Dreaming centres. The Aborigines, if they are asked, can draw detailed and careful maps of their own country and that of their neighbours, marking every important site. Next to travelling all through the tribal territories, examining each hill and billabong, yam patch and kangaroo hunting ground, and every sacred place, collecting such maps gives us the best broad idea of what these lands are like from the point of view of the people who live in them.

Over the centuries, even before white contact, there must have been much moving about and changing of boundaries until the tribes finally settled down into their own more or less elastic compartments. But the true tribal country is that in which the great Ancestral Beings travelled and had their adventures, introducing rituals and ceremonies, creating the landscape as we know it to-day. Through these Beings, as Professor A. P. Elkin has so ably shown in his *Australian Aborigines*, each man, woman and child has a strong and even passionate bond with his own country, the 'eternal' home of his spirits. People may fight and kill one another: but the land never changes hands. Given to the tribe long ago in mythological times, it is something fixed and immutable, not to be quarrelled over and divided by men.

Nearly every tribe had a name for itself, though sometimes the meaning was lost in the mists of the past. Often, like the Dieri of Lake Eyre, the name simply meant 'man'—as opposed to the lesser human beings of other tribes. But there were others too, like the Walang or Gunbalang, the 'Bat' people living among the caves on the northern Arnhem Land coast; the Maijali or 'Stone country' people south of Oenpelli; the Gunwinggu or Winggu, 'fresh water', people of western Arnhem Land; the Lungga or 'Long Faced' people of west-central Northern Territory.

A few tribes once lived in relative isolation, intolerant of their neighbours' ideas, marrying and rearing their children within their own boundaries. On occasions they joined with others for trading purposes, or in the big religious ceremonies: but for the most part they were virtually self-contained. This complete reliance on their own resources, this emotional dependence on their conventional background, made it much harder for them to adjust themselves to the ultimate contact with aliens which they could not evade nor ignore.

Other tribes, sharing a common heritage of language and tradition, have formed loose and often vague alliances. They marry together; go more or less freely through one another's tribal lands; help one another economically; and combine to perform religious or even secular ceremonies. The best known of these is the Pidjandja-speaking bloc, with combined territories extending across the Great Victoria Desert and through the Musgrave and Everard Ranges, up the Canning Stock route, and into the Wailbri and Waneiga country about Tanami and the Granites. On the lower River Murray a century ago was the so-called 'Narrinyeri' Confederacy, numbering among its tribes the Wakend, Tangani, Jaraldi, Tatiera and Ramindjeri. Then there are the 'Bringkin' groups on the north coast of Australia, between the Daly River and the Fitzmaurice, today gradually diminishing in number as they drift into the white man's settlements.

The tribe is a territorial and linguistic unit, of little importance politically or economically. It rarely functions as a whole in warfare and feuding, food-gathering and hunting. These are matters which concern smaller groups —the clan, the horde, or the family unit.

Members of a clan trace common descent, sometimes through the father (as in eastern Arnhem Land), sometimes through the mother (as in western Arnhem Land). They belong to a special district within the tribal territory, and sometimes have their own special rituals or songs. But members of a clan should not inter-marry. They find their wives and husbands in other clans, often within the same tribe; and this extended family group of parents and children, frequently with other relatives as well, is the horde.

Another feature of Aboriginal life is what anthropologists call a moiety. Nearly all over Australia, every tribe was divided theoretically into two halves for social and ceremonial purposes. Usually a man should not marry within his own moiety, but must look for a wife in one of the clans of the opposite moiety: and his children may belong to either his grouping or that of their mother, according to the local way of reckoning descent. This division is often extended to embrace all people, creatures and things in heaven and earth, so that it is also partly totemic in nature.

Sometimes the moieties themselves are divided into sections or sub-sections to provide special marriage rules, and group various relatives in different ways.

The social organization of these Aborigines is not a simple matter, easily grasped by the outsider. It is complicated and often abstruse, full of hidden difficulties and contradictions: but to the people themselves, who have absorbed it since childhood, mastering its secrets, it is merely part of the ordinary fabric of everyday life.

A stylized representation of a woman; a drawing used in sorcery; from Oenpelli, western Arnhem Land.

CHAPTER IV

Making a Living

MAN, wherever he finds himself, needs more than his bare hands to help him survive. So the Aborigines too, like people everywhere, were obliged to invent various tools and weapons for hunting and food-collecting. Through the ages these were altered to suit their needs, and supplemented by others; the invention of the spearthrower, for instance, was a discovery of major importance. And each object was developed to the limit of its usefulness, made as nearly perfect as possible.

Because of the way they live, paying far less attention than we do to material objects, the Aborigines carry with them only what they feel to be vitally necessary. To ensure that he and his family have enough to eat, all a man needs in the bush are a spearthrower and a handful of spears. He knows intimately all the habits of the creatures around him, for without this knowledge his spears and his skill would be useless. He must track with stealth, reading the sometimes scanty evidence left by his quarry, imitate the sounds of animals and birds, understand the directions of the wind and the importance of the seasons in hunting. These are only a few of the accomplishments he needs. Even where bush foods are plentiful, along the coasts and some of the large rivers, or during good seasons in the hills around Ernabella in Central Australia, he must have both knowledge and skill, developed and maintained through continual practice.

The coastal and river people make fishing spears, lines with bone or wooden hooks, and turtle or dugong harpoons with wooden buoys attached to mark the site of the kill. They have rafts, stringy-bark canoes sewn with fibre, and along the Murray and Darling Rivers canoes from tree-trunks and hollow logs. The northern coastal tribes made log canoes only after contact with Indonesians: but some of them are beautifully shaped, and much more elaborate than those of the South: they have cut-in ridges for seats, incised or painted paddles, and Macassan-type sails once woven from pandanus fibre. A canoe dipping home under sail against the sunset, and dragged up on the beach through the rosy breakers, is a sight that lingers long in the memory.

River canoes, in contrast with those used on the open sea, need sharp prows which can cleave their way through the grasses, lilies and weeds of the billabongs and shallow streams. Inland, too, people make rafts of bark, bamboo or saplings to ferry themselves across the rivers, or along the pools and waterways after heavy rains.

Aboriginal fisherfolk used to build traps of stones, and ingenious barriers of grass, brush or logs, for catching fish as the waters receded. The north-eastern Arnhem Landers, and tribes of the Daly River, in good seasons often found themselves with more fish than they could eat. They would make, too, nets of large or small mesh, drag-nets, or large drum nets fastened to buoys.

40

To carry fish and other foods, women would plait baskets and dilly bags of pandanus fibre, or various reeds or grasses. Some of them are woven tightly enough to hold water or honey over long distances. Other tribes use kangaroo skins for water, wooden and bark dishes, or huge baler shells: and some of the Coorong people in South Australia used human skulls.

Articles made by the Aborigines are many and varied: boomerangs, fighting clubs, wedges, chisels, incising tools, stones for grinding and polishing. Today the stone axe is rarely used, for the steel tomahawk has taken its place. But it was a good tool, made usually of dark basalt, with a smooth edge sharpened by constant grinding and able to cut through the hardest wood. There are emu-feather fans and fly-whisks, long carved pipes, and a host of different spears—barbed, painted, poison-tipped, iron-bladed: spears of bamboo or wood, for fishing, hunting or fighting. In the Kimberleys and west central Northern Territory, flaked spear-heads are still made from tapering quartzite, carefully chipped and flaked, and mounted on long straight shafts.

Their huts are varied, too: of stringy-bark or paper-bark, sometimes roofed with a smearing of clay: mosquito huts, or stilted wet season huts for the flooding billabongs of the coastal flats. Some tribes camp from time to time in the caves of their rocky hills, but mostly, in dry weather, they use light windbreaks of leafy boughs. There is always a fire burning, filling the air with sweet wood smoke: and everywhere, all over the camp, are the inevitable dogs.

So often the Aborigine is dismissed as a feckless, improvident simpleton, living for the day with 'no thought of the morrow'. But he does not hoard food, any more than we would hoard meat if we lived near a butcher and had no refrigerator at home. Like most of us, he prefers

41

his food to be fresh; and so he obtains it at frequent intervals to suit his needs.

In parts of Australia, though, some foods are preserved. In the Great Victoria Desert quondongs, wild peaches, are dried in the sun and kept for some time; and the northern Arnhem Landers used to smoke-dry green plums, which they pounded and used for damper. Beside the Lower River Murray in the early days, and near the Stirling River in the Northern Territory, various fish were smoked and dried; and the Daly River tribes can preserve shark-meat for several days, by squeezing it dry and packing it tightly in leaves.

The Aborigines in their Bush home make use of all the available natural resources, adapting themselves almost perfectly to their surroundings. They know where and at what time of the year to find all the foods that grow in their natural gardens, and are careful never to spoil a plant by over-picking. Thus they do not collect all the roots of a yam plant, but leave some to bear again in the following season.

From long experience they know what is edible and what is not, and what must be treated before it is safe to eat. They can cook their foods so that none of the value is lost, keeping their proper flavour as well. And all over the world they are famed for their skill in finding fresh water; in dry regions, however barren the prospects may seem to the stranger, in hollow trees, in frogs which have stored their water supply within their bodies, and in native soaks and wells.

With deceptive ease, they can live and thrive in country where the white man, for all his superior techniques, would perish. But this is no matter of instinct, of almost automatic adjustment. Years of training go to make the adept hunter, acquainted with every inch of his own land.

In many places, a man regards his spear as virtually a

part of himself. It is rarely out of his hands, and even when he is resting or dancing it is always nearby in case of emergency. Wherever he goes, he must carry it ready for use, and for this he needs freedom of action; he must not be hampered by children, by bundles and baskets of food or belongings. So, when people are moving camp, it is quite common to see a man lightly bearing his spears and weapons, while behind him follow the women and children, heavily laden. Thoughtless observers have jumped to the conclusion that Aboriginal woman leads a life of drudgery, bullied and put upon by her menfolk. But this is far from being the case.

Men and women co-operate in making the best use of their energy and natural resources.

For the most part, men carry out the most spectacular tasks: the stalking and killing of kangaroos, the spearing of fish, the catching of turtle. These demand greater vigour, and sudden bursts of activity. Women often have young children to mind, and cannot walk fast. They spread their work over the whole day, usually going in parties, where each gathers food for her family. They collect wild fruits—black or green plums, wild apples or peaches: long sweet yams, or bitter roots that need special treatment: stems and roots of the blue or red water lily, or seeds to be crushed for damper: 'possums and bandicoots: witchetty grubs, honey ants, and various nuts. Or they go down to the sea and get shell fish, oysters and mussels, or big mangrove crabs to be cooked on the coals.

Men may dig yams too, if they wish, and women sometimes kill wallabies. And either may collect eggs, or kill goanna or snakes, or find a wild bees' nest and extract the sweet, dark honey. But for the most part men bring home the larger meats and fish, and women the smaller.

When a man comes back to camp with an emu or kangaroo, he keeps only enough for his own family. All

43

the rest is shared among various relatives, or people to whom he is under some obligation. He has his wife's parents to think of, as well as his own: his brothers, and grandparents, or distant and only nominal kin. Sometimes he has special commitments: all the meat may be put aside for the dancers and songmen in one of the big ceremonies, or kept for the elders.

But often, in bad seasons, a man may return empty-handed day after day, while his wife nearly always comes back with something—a few berries or tubers, some bull-rush roots or a handful of water peanuts. Her work is more of a routine kind, less dependent on factors of chance; and so, whatever success or failure a man may have in his hunting, the family relies in the long run largely on what the woman provides.

There are no drones in an Aboriginal community. Elders and certain ceremonial headmen, or tribal specialists, expect others to help maintain them: but we must remember that they are contributing something to the community, or to some of its members, and so they demand some material recompense. In the same way, a native doctor who heals the sick is usually paid for his services. Old people, too, who can no longer forage for food will be looked after by their kin. But no man fritters away the passing hours in dreaming or sleeping, while his wife works; and no woman remains idle all her life, kept by her husband. Food-collecting is part of the ordinary course of life for all able-bodied men and women.

The Aboriginal boy is taught to hunt and obtain meat, the girl to collect seeds and fruits, yams and small animals; and they learn how food must be shared throughout the camp, according to friendship and kinship ties. The boy finds out that if he is to marry, and play his part in community life, he must know how to handle his weapons and develop his hunting abilities. Long before his betrothed wife comes to his camp to sleep, he must supply her parents with food. It is not sufficient to obtain just enough for himself. He must consider others as well; and then he, in turn, can expect to receive favours from them.

Again mythology comes into the picture, giving meaning and sanction to the whole arrangement of economic life. It was the Ancestral Beings who provided all these foods, and first advised people how to collect them: and they are responsible now for keeping up the supply. Almost every feature has a mythological basis, from the semi-religious increase ceremonies, partly magical, to the sale or exchange of songs and stories, rituals and chants.

Decorated dilly-bags or baskets from Western Arnhem Land.

CHAPTER V

Trade

OFTEN, ritual and economics are linked so closely
that the one could not function without the other.
In the trade ceremonies of western Arnhem Land
various tribes assemble together not merely to lose themselves in the dancing and singing, but also to obtain goods
they need or desire. The value of these goods is always
enhanced by the rituals, and the actual exchange comes
as a vivid climax to weeks of anticipation.

Ordinary life is interrupted, and all the camps have an
air of excitement and holiday. People must eat, of course,
and go out hunting from time to time: but for days in
advance they have gathered foods that will last for a
while without spoiling—seeds and nuts, roots and various
eggs: meat to be hung on trees away from the dogs: or
living goannas and fresh-water tortoises, kept until they
are wanted.

Everyone is in the mood for enjoyment. Not only
goods are exchanged, but ideas as well: and people take
the opportunity not only to settle differences but also

to make new friends. They arrange betrothals and marriages, gossip and dance and make love—for ordinary rules are relaxed, and all but the oldest and youngest can take what sweethearts they please.

The western Arnhem Landers have six principal trade ceremonies, each associated with a certain area. In one of these, the *djamalag*, the emphasis is on sexual licence, but this does not detract from the importance of the economic exchange and the consolidating of intertribal friendships. It culminates in the ritual presentation of trade goods, such as the shovel-bladed or serrated spears from the east.

In another, the *rom*, distinctive emblems are sent to summon the visitors, who perform special dances of a totemic nature before the final exchange. The *midjan* introduces a different series of dances relating to the sea coast. The visitors have prepared hanks of twine from hair belonging to their hosts, and for this they receive payment in goods. In the *wurbu* series people are more interested in obtaining special breast mats and baskets: and the concluding rituals, where eggs are presented in the trade exchange after the dancing, seem to be connected with the idea of magical increase. Then there is the *mamurung*: but this has no special dancing, and most of its songs deal with present-day life. Most spectacular of all is the *njalaidj*, which bears close resemblance to the beautiful sacred dancing of the *kunapipi*. It is commemorated in many myths: for the *njalaidj* traders brought the highly valued red ochres used in cave paintings, and the special stone spears which only they could make.

On the Daly River, south-west of Darwin, goods are handed over in a more matter of fact way when neighbouring tribes have gathered for other reasons—initiation or various sacred ceremonies. Here, as in north-eastern

Arnhem Land, each man or woman has a special trading partner in a complex network of gift exchange.

All over Aboriginal Australia there was a vast criss-crossing of trade routes, along which passed articles of recognized value. From the north-west, about the Kimberleys, pearl-shells were traded down as far as the Nullabor Plain.

Native tobacco came down from the central ranges, and wombat fur for twine came up from the south. In Arnhem Land, stone spear heads are traded from inland quarries; and red-ochre, human hair belts and beautifully painted and feathered bags are passed from one tribe to another.

Today, all this elaborate pattern is almost destroyed. Tribes who still maintain it, on the northern coast and the inland 'deserts', have introduced new items of alien significance—beads and tobacco, clothing and knives; blankets, coloured wools, and bright cotton cloth.

As long as people in one place have what is needed by others with no means of getting it, this trade will continue. But many commodities now come direct from the white man, while goods like opossum fur twine and flaked-glass spearheads are steadily losing their prestige value. Probably, in years to come, trading between the tribes will follow other features of Aboriginal life into oblivion.

15. Playing at cat's-cradles or string figures, depicting everyday and mythic themes. Amata, Musgrave Ranges, 1967.
Photograph: courtesy N. M. Wallace

16. Boy being painted by his mother's brother for the first time with *ili* Dreaming designs. Near Amata, Musgrave Ranges, 1970.
Photograph: courtesy N. M. Wallace

Left: 17. Girl carrying water in wooden dish. Owellinna (Awalana) spring, Musgrave Ranges, 1940.
Photograph: courtesy C. P. Mountford

Below: 18. Getting water from Owellinna spring, Musgrave Ranges, 1940.
Photograph: courtesy C. P. Mountford

19. Drinking from Kalaia-tjunda (emu-thigh) rockhole. Ayers Rock, Central Australia, 1940. It was here that the mythic Sleepy Lizard man cooked emu.
Photograph: courtesy C. P. Mountford

20. Returning to camp after collecting food. Gibson Desert, 1967.
Photograph: courtesy I. Dunlop

21. Carrying an emu back t
camp; a small boy follows
his father. Gibson Desert,
1967.
Photograph: courtesy I. Dunlop

22. Getting water from a
well, I. Gibson Desert,
1967.
Photograph: courtesy I. Dunlop

23. Getting water from a
well, II. Gibson Desert,
1967.
Photograph: courtesy I. Dunlop

CHAPTER VI

Growing Up

A^N Aboriginal baby at birth is light in colour: but after a few days only the palms of his hands and the soles of his feet remain that way. Helpless and small as he is, already he is a member of his clan and tribe, with his own totem and spirit home, his own place in the life of his people. But until he is old enough to have sense he must be cared for, and taught how to behave.

His mother and his 'other mothers', her sisters; his grandparents and his father's sisters: all help to look after him, to feed him with breast-milk and small soft pieces of food that he can easily swallow. He learns to ride on their shoulders, perhaps, clutching their hair: and sometimes he falls asleep astride his mother's neck of an evening, as she shuffles in time to the clapping and singing.

People try to teach him to talk. They laugh and play with him, petting and teasing him, saying the same words over and over again until he repeats them. Soon he knows his own mother and father, and what to call them:

49

and he can say simple words—although at first nobody knows what he is trying to tell them.

In some tribes, his mother or father may stand a stick upright in the ground beside the camp, and this keeps him happy for hours. He uses it to pull himself up; he stands, holding it; he takes little steps around it; and at last he can leave the stick and run by himself. Now he is old enough to play with toy spears or boomerangs, trying to behave like a man; and a little girl may try to copy what she has seen the women doing. They give her a tiny basket, or a small wooden dish, filling it perhaps with pieces of cooked food to make her feel important.

Until they are about four years old, children are not expected to take in very much of what they hear. In fact, they are sometimes present during deeply religious discussions between elders and initiated men, when older children would be driven away or punished.

But as soon as a child can walk and run, his grandfather or grandmother, or other people about him, will sing to him and start teaching him a few of the simplest dance steps. He is used to the rhythms already, for even babies of less than a year old are dandled and gently bounced about to the beat of the singing: and now they show him how to control his limbs and gradually prepare for more elaborate movements.

Some of the songs he learns are sung by adults as well. But in many places there are traditional children's songs, happy little snatches of rhythm about spirits or animals, or the birds and other creatures he sees about him. These songs are only a preliminary, a starting point in the long process of learning and growing: for during his early years he is preparing to take his place as a fully equipped member of his community.

A child with no young brother or sister can run to his mother's breast whenever he feels hungry or thirsty: but

usually he is weaned in one way or another before he is
five or six. Then a little boy often leaves his parents'
windbreak or hut to camp with playmates about his own
age.

Small boys and girls may play separately. The girls
cluster together to imitate mourners about a corpse,
wailing and gashing their heads, or pretend to be grown
women searching for yams and fruits or witchetty grubs.
The boys go hunting together, spearing lizards or birds,
or engage in mock fights. In north-eastern Arnhem Land
two bands of small boys will gather a hundred yards or
so apart, singing defiant songs to get themselves into the
right mood before suddenly rushing at each other with
showers of toy spears. Then there is a wild scatter as
mothers and grannies come scolding to snatch them up:
for these little spears are dangerous, with their sharp
points of glass or bamboo, and now and then children
have been blinded or killed.

Even in play, children are learning ways that will help
them in adult life. They join in their own ceremonies,
the girls dancing perhaps while the boys sing, or other
small boys stamp and leap while the young spectators
shrilly applaud them. Or they play 'husband and wife',
with maybe a sweetheart or two to complicate the picture,
and children to cuddle and scold.

All over Australia, the Aborigines have been fond of
children—even in 'desert' places where they had to
practise infanticide during droughts and times of star-
vation. They pet and spoil a child, allowing him all
kinds of liberties: but just as often they will turn at last,
thoroughly exasperated, and punish him harshly. They
are not always consistent. Nevertheless, by the time he
reaches puberty, he has a fair idea of what is expected
of him.

By that time, perhaps, he may have had his nasal septum pierced: for in some tribes this is done to girls and boys about nine or ten years old. He may have been circumcised, too, as happens at seven or eight in northeastern Arnhem Land; but in central Australia and most other parts he must wait till he is fourteen or sixteen, or even older.

A girl at puberty usually goes through certain rituals that mark her new status of womanhood, sometimes with physical operations as well. A few of the northern coastal tribes have quite elaborate rituals. The girl is a striking figure as she comes out of seclusion, smeared with red ochre and brightly decorated, her white forehead band shining. At the climax, all the women escort her at dawn to a fresh water stream or lagoon; and even the oldest among them forget their age as they splash and sing in the shallows.

But on the whole, the ceremonies that surround a boy are longer, and more spectacular. Once he reaches adolescence, he knows that he will soon be initiated. Maybe he feels a little frightened, reluctant to face the ordeal: but at the same time he knows that this is his way of reaching adulthood. It shows that he is nearly ready to marry, to assume his family and religious responsibilities. This expectation colours his whole approach to everyday life. He pays close attention to the actions of his elders, for some slight unintentional sign on their part may give a clue to the time of his initiation. He may wish to stay more with his mother and female relatives. But outwardly, and especially to his friends, he is either impatient for the whole business to start, or boasts rather halfheartedly that the 'old men won't catch him'.

In any case, he nearly always accepts the process as a matter of course. He wants to be a man, to marry and have children of his own: to be taught the sacred doctrines, and take a full part in totemic cult life. If he has not been wild in his childhood: if he has listened to his elders, learnt the songs and steps he was taught: if he is sensible and can remember what he is told: if his spear is straight, and he shows some patience and skill as a hunter: then he may not have to wait long for the first rites. But if he has been cheeky and ill-behaved, so that the old men dislike him, he may be kept in suspense for some time.

Initiation rituals vary from tribe to tribe, each with its own associated mythology.

Some non-circumcising groups prefer depilation, removal of body or facial hair—the Maung of Goulburn Islands, the Bathurst and Melville Islanders, and the people who once lived on the lower Murray. Some practise the blood rite, anointing the novice with blood or red ochre: or tooth avulsion, loosening and tapping out one or two middle teeth in the upper jaw. Then there is the tossing rite, widely found, or the throwing of fire over the heads of the novices. Cicatrization or scarring may be practised too, though not always as a part of initiation.

But in nearly all tribes, circumcision was the focal point of the whole initiation—or at least of the first rituals. Sometimes it is followed, a few years after puberty, by subincision. This is associated with very important rituals, divided into special stages; and later on the incisure will be opened again every time the right ceremonies are held.

Very broadly speaking, there are two patterns of meaning, both related. In the first, initiation follows the theme of death—a symbolic enactment of dying and rising again from the dead. Some tribes say that the young boy, taken from the main camp, is swallowed by an Ancestral Spirit, who finally vomits him up to return to life as a new being. In the second, he returns to the womb of the Fertility Mother; he passes through various rituals; his foreskin is cut to symbolize the severing of the umbilical

53

cord; and then, re-born, he again comes back to the camp.

From the point of view of the tribe, the novice, through a complicated system of discipline and teaching (often symbolically expressed), is being made a full member of the society. He does not learn everything at his initiation. A man, like a woman, is adding all through his life to his knowledge of sacred ritual: and he may be quite old before the final revelations are disclosed to him. Initiation merely opens the door to full adulthood, to the sacred life of his group.

After his final initiation, he may marry; the men who circumcised him may be obliged to give him a wife, and in some tribes he need not wait till after his subincision. Quite possibly, a certain girl was promised to him as a baby; and now she will come to him; or if she has not reached puberty he will 'rear her', providing her and her parents with food. He is now, officially speaking, an adult, with all an adult's responsibilities.

Nevertheless, only when he marries and perhaps has a child does the rest of the community really regard him as a fully grown man; and this is true for a woman as well. Marriage gives stability to them both, and enhances their prestige. Parenthood is expected of them; and where the delicate balance of tribal life has not been drastically shaken it usually follows naturally, with no special ceremony to mark the birth. But this does not mean that no-one is interested. A child is a new man or a new woman, one in spirit with all of his clan or tribe; and the birth of a first baby, especially, represents a crisis in the life of his parents—his father no less than his mother.

When a man reaches middle-age he may, through his outstanding personality, become a camp boss or headman. Among some people, such as the Pidjandja-speaking tribes, he may become a native doctor, able to practise special forms of sorcery as well as of healing; but to become a doctor, in most parts of Australia, a man must undergo another initiation, linked with long and careful training. Occasionally, though not in all tribes, a woman too may be a doctor: but usually they are men.

Later still, at about fifty or sixty, he becomes an elder. Everyone has a voice in the affairs of family and tribe: but formal decisions are often made by the older men, led by the headman of their choice.

As his hunting ability declines, he comes to rely more and more on gifts from his sons-in-law, and his own sons. Now he and his wife are reaping the advantage of having children, who will look after them in their old age; and if he has a young wife or two, as well as an old one, they have an energetic domestic help to attend to their comforts.

In the ordinary course of events, he is anxious to hand on to worthy recipients as much of the old ways as he can. He is an upholder of tradition, a conservative force in the community, and a mine of information concerning all the ritual, mythology and song he has absorbed over the years.

Old men and women are rarely neglected or badly treated. Nearly everywhere, adequate food comes to them by reason of kinship and marriage obligations, without grudging or reluctance. Where the white man has not undermined the prestige of age and experience, they are respected and looked up to; and grey hair is a sign not of uselessness and decay, but of knowledge and wisdom.

CHAPTER VII

The Cycle of Life

FOR these First Australians, life begins as it ends—
with the spirit.

The first life crisis comes when the child's soul, through
the mystic experience of its father or one of his relatives,
leaves its totemic centre or spirit home and enters the
chosen mother, who already has within her the material
substance in which it will dwell.

Next, for a boy, comes the initiation or the age-grading
rites—which may stretch into a series of crises punctuating
his youth. The counterpart for a girl is puberty and its
associated rituals, often colourful and always socially
significant.

Mechanisms of age-grading superficially divide the
men from the women, on the basis of those who take
part or are initiated into certain ceremonies. Nevertheless,
there is no sharp cleavage between the two, at this or at
any other ritual stage. Men and women both have their
separate parts to play, and both are of equal importance.

Through age-grading or puberty rites, or some kind of

initiation, comes the passage from childhood to near-adulthood.

Now the girl may go to her husband, if she is not living with him already: and after a time she too will bear children to follow in the same pattern. Of course, she still has a great deal to learn: but as a rule this comes to her informally, without the definite stages that mark the life of a boy.

For him, the series of rites he goes through marks his gradual acceptance as a practising member of the most important cults known to his tribe. How far he is able to develop this interest depends on the force of traditional life, on the strength of his religious convictions, and the capability of his teachers.

The Aborigine, male or female, is a complex and many-sided social personality. He is a member not only of his small immediate family, but also of larger and less closely personal units—the clan, the tribe, the linguistic group, the moiety; he belongs to a totemic system, a scheme of mythology, ceremony and belief, in which he feels a direct and active responsibility.

As the years of childhood pass, and he takes an increasing share in community life, so he becomes incorporated more and more fully into the Aboriginal Way, in all its varied aspects.

To begin with, the essence of man or woman is purely spiritual. After birth, exposed to the rude conditions of workaday life, it takes on a materialistic form: but it never loses its sacred quality. Woman possesses this sacredness almost without any effort—especially in such places as north-eastern Arnhem Land; but for man the accent is on ritual, and organized ceremony. For both, sacredness increases with advancing age; and at death they become, again, completely spiritual.

CHAPTER VIII

Men and Women

WHAT of the people themselves—the men and women whose life before white contact was bounded by the confines of this narrow world? How did they respond, individually, to the conventions that governed all their speech and their actions?

We are accustomed to thinking of an Aboriginal culture in rather more general terms. When we look at the social organization and kinship rules, the technology, the economic structure and religious beliefs, the individual man or woman seems to be obscured, merged into the composite picture of his group as a whole. But no matter how successful the learning processes of his society, no matter how passively he seems to conform, he must always retain something that is personal and unique to himself. Subject in this classless society to the same controls and pressures, the same types of experience, as all his neighbours, he yet does not respond in exactly the same way. In each man and woman lies the power to deviate, however infinitesimally, from dictated patterns.

Thus in theory a man should marry only a woman who stands in a special relationship to him: but although most marriages seem to follow this rule, there are and have been many which do not. Provided the union is not regarded as incest, the rest of the community does not as a rule make serious trouble. Then there is the strong tabu between a man and his mother-in-law or any of her tribal sisters. Except during periods of ceremonial licence, these two are usually forbidden to speak to or even approach each other; but even this strict prohibition has been circumvented at times.

When sacred ceremonies are in progress, not everyone entitled to take part may do so; some men and women are always more enthusiastic than others. Some try to learn and understand as much as they can of mythology and ritual behaviour: others take only the most perfunctory interest. Some enjoy singing and dancing, doing so happily at the least opportunity: but the singing of others is flat and tuneless, their movements awkward and lacking in grace. In some tribes a man may, if he wishes, have several wives at a time: but just as often he prefers to confine himself to one. Another man or woman may be dissatisfied with the limitations of marriage, and constantly try to find satisfaction outside it. Some men delight in composing songs: while others are content to accept what tradition and their contemporaries provide.

So within every tribe no two people are quite alike. There are women who take loving care of their husbands and children, and women whose domestic efforts are reluctant and sketchy. There are quiet men devoted to their wives, and men who believe in using their weapons to keep peace in the family. There are wives who do meekly what they are told, and wives whose biting tongues are notorious far beyond their home camps.

Old Ngalmanagu[7] for instance, at Oenpelli, has a

reputation for speaking her mind. Thin and sharp-featured, deceptively mild of manner, she drinks in news of the latest scandals: and victims, when she is roused, shrink from her caustic comments. In girlhood she married her present husband; and now, a grandmother, she is his only surviving wife. Even he, say his friends (though he will not admit it), is afraid of her tongue: for she has no hesitation in opposing him publicly during a camp quarrel. A rougher man might have curbed her hasty temper by force, or offered her in marriage to some-one else: but within her own family she is just as in-dustrious and affectionate as her neighbours, and both she and her husband seem to take the permanency of their marriage for granted.

Then there is old Mureimurei of the eastern Arnhem Land coast. She is a frail and gentle great-grandmother now: but even in her youth, we are told, she was much less self-assertive than the other women about her. In childhood she was betrothed to Wonggu, and came to him as his first wife. As he gathered one more woman after another into his household she accepted them all, with at least outward docility. Maybe she felt that her place was secure, with three daughters and three strong sons: but she did not boldly assert her rights, jockeying as the others did for the position of favourite, or quarrelling over the distribution of meat and fish which their husband brought home.

Kamal, the wife of her sister's son, does not share her viewpoint. Her kin betrothed her early to Maijamaija, and she went obediently to his camp. But Maijamaija already had a number of wives: and Kamal, spirited and quick like her old mother at Milingimbi, did not like the arrangement. 'We were always fighting,' she says: 'and he couldn't get enough meat for us all.' So one night she crept from the camp, leaving her two little girls behind. Mau was visiting Milingimbi just then, and they were already sweethearts. Stealthily she awakened him and persuaded him to take her home with him in his canoe, tied up on the beach nearby. By morning, when Mai-jamaija discovered his loss, she was well away on the long journey to Yirrkalla. For years afterwards Kamal was afraid to visit her parents: but Maijamaija had so many wives, that one here or there did not matter. Now, with her second family growing up, and newly a grandmother, Kamal has encountered her first problem again: for Mau had two young girls promised to him as wives, and was anxious for them to join her. She fought this proposal bitterly, with threats and persuasion and violence—everything, in fact, short of leaving him. At last, more than ten years after marrying Mau, she has yielded to circumstances rather than lose him; but her pride and self-respect are salved by the new authority she can wield, and no one in her camp may forget that she is Mau's first and his chief wife.

Milngari from the Stirling River, impatient and over-bearing, proud of the ceremonies which appeared to her in a trance: Miangula from the Tanami 'deserts', with a mop of chestnut hair, and a complacent husband who encourages her to consort with white men: young Lamanga of the Arnhem Land coast, notorious for the number and frequency of her lovers: young or old, each has her own store of experience, her peculiarities of behaviour which set her apart from the rest.

So it is, too, with the men.

There is the patriarch Wonggu of north-eastern Arnhem Land, who as a young man had dealings with Indonesian traders at Caledon Bay. Shrewd and aggressive, he built up his prestige and wealth until men of neighbouring clans were more than willing to give him their daughters. Soon his ties of influence stretched in every direction, becoming stronger and broader as his daughters were strategically married, and his sons grew to manhood adding fresh spears to his service. He was a fighter and killer, likening himself to the shark which symbolizes his clan, and relying on force or bluff to achieve his desires. Shipwrecked travellers, or small bands of Japanese pearlers, fell victim to his planning: but when the white men came he did not oppose them, finding it wiser to trade, or to barter his womenfolk for their goods. With his materialistic bias he has never paid much attention to ceremonial affairs. From his father he inherited ceremonial leadership of his clan: but although he can provide generously at feasts, and fulfil ritual obligations with ease, he prefers to delegate much of his responsibility to a few of his clansfolk. Now that he is old, and the introduced laws prohibit the fighting he once enjoyed, he relies heavily on his sons. But these men too, though still a little in awe of him, are accustomed to having their own way: and so, unknown to their father, they have chosen sweethearts among his younger wives, whom they plan to marry as soon as he dies.

Mauwulan, of Yirrkalla, has had only three wives instead of the twenty-two which Wonggu gathered about him. An expert hunter and fighter, alive to his own interests, he preferred to concentrate on religious and ritual matters rather than on trading and accumulating wealth. He is an expert on the mythology and songs of his clan, an authority on ritual and law: and his wives, like Wonggu's, have enjoyed the reflection of his prestige. With it all, he is a family man, grieving bitterly over the death of his old wife Bamadja, and finding constant delight in spoiling and displaying his little daughter.

'Wogiman Paddy', as the Daly River settlers call him, is different. Past middle age, he is a religious fanatic, trying to revive indigenous rituals in an area long disturbed by European contact. He travels along the River and far afield, bringing old ceremonies to life and instigating new ones.

In many parts of Australia there are such outstanding men who catch and hold the attention, making their fellows by contrast appear mediocre and uninspired. Kokalalja of Birrundudu, also a ceremonial leader, a commanding figure as he travels through the north-central 'deserts': nobody dares to begin a sacred ritual, when he is about, until he makes his appearance; Mushabin of Ooldea, Mungguldjungul of Tanami—to them, as to others, interest in ceremonial affairs has brought personal satisfaction, and enhanced status within their group.

Then there is Guningbal of western Arnhem Land, a young man still but a famous composer of 'gossip' songs. Or white haired Midjaumidjau of Oenpelli, a skilful artist whose ochred lines on a stringybark canvas are a constant delight to the eye. Or Bababa of the Great Victoria Desert, a powerful native doctor, with the tiny bag of his profession fastened safely among the grey hairs of his beard.

Men and women of varied talents and interests, some of them more outstanding, more vivid than others, but all individual personalities in their own right: together, on a common framework which all of them share, with a thousand and one threads they build up the complex pattern of their society.

The tongues of the Lightning Snakes flicker and twist,
    one to the other . . .
They flash among the foliage of the cabbage palms . . .
Lightning flashes through the clouds, with the flickering
    tongue of the Snake . . .
It is always there, at the wide expanse of water,
    at the place of the sacred tree . . .
Flashing above those people of the western clans,
All over the sky their tongues flicker: above the place of the
    Rising Clouds, the place of the Standing Clouds,
All over the sky, tongues flickering and twisting . . .
They are always there, at the camp by the wide expanse
    of water . . .
All over the sky their tongues flicker: at the place of
    the Two Sisters, the place of the Wauwalak.
Lightning flashes through the clouds, flash of the
    Lightning Snake . . .
Its blinding flash lights up the cabbage palm foliage . . .
Gleams on the cabbage palms, and on the shining leaves . . .

(Song No. 21 of the 'Goulburn Island' Love Cycle, from north-
eastern Arnhem Land. The Lightning Snakes play across the sky
at the beginning of the monsoonal period.)

24. Beside a windbreak, a woman (with her son) separates edible seeds from husk. Gibson Desert, 1965.
Photograph: courtesy I. Dunlop

25. A child watches his father making a spearthrower. Gibson Desert, 1965.
Photograph: courtesy I. Dunlop

26. Traditionally-oriented Bindubi people sitting in the shade at Walawala, Western Desert, 1964.
Photograph: courtesy B. Tonkinson

27. Five bushmen at Dadiwara, Western Desert, 1964.
Photograph: courtesy B. Tonkinson

28. Equipped for the daily round of food collection. A Desert woman carries a dish on her head, made stable by a pad, and holds a digging stick. She is about to collect seeds from a clump of grass to her right.
Photograph : courtesy B. Tonkinson

Left: 29. Examining bush tobacco—which is chewed not smoked. This particular variety is found in sandhill areas of the Western Desert. Behind is a fine specimen of a desert oak.
Photograph: courtesy B. Tonkinson

Below: 30. Gutting a kangaroo in readiness for cooking. Western Desert, 1964-65. Note swarms of flies, an ordinary accompaniment of Desert living.
Photograph: courtesy B. Tonkinson

CHAPTER IX

The Meaning of Life

SACRED ritual and ceremony, striking and vivid—
how much has been written about them! The white
stranger coming into the camps, as into a different world,
could watch with fascinated or disapproving gaze the
intent dancers, fantastically decorated with feathers and
coloured ochres. He could see and record their steps, the
fierce intensity of their movements, the exultation of
their singing and posturing. The shell, the husk, of it all
was his for the taking. The 'kangaroo' dance, the acting
out of the sacred goanna myth, the rites of blood-letting
and subincision—he could label them all, perhaps, these
glimpses into the soul of a people.

But what of their meaning? Why should adult men
and women throw themselves, with almost fanatical
passion, into these rites that seem to the outsider so
weird and bizarre, childish play-acting devoid of deep
significance?

So hard it is for us, lacking the key, to enter into the
emotion and faith of people with whom we have no

shared experience, no common religious doctrine. Observation alone is not enough. We must try to understand what it is that makes them vital and real, what breathes life and purpose into these gestures and rituals which we cannot fit into our own framework of meaning.

There is totemism, for instance, a concept foreign to our way of thinking. A close spiritual bond linking man with nature in all its aspects, it has no counterpart in our own philosophy. Yet among so many of the Aborigines it is the logical expression of their relation to their environment, where man is not spiritually a being apart, but springs from the same source as all other forms of life in the universe as he knows it: and past, present and future are merged into one 'eternal' reality. Totemism, then, is a view of life, reflecting the essential unity of all living things and all natural forces: but man, in his opinion, is always the central figure.

In all its varied manifestations, it runs like a cohesive thread through every feature of Aboriginal life. Groups of men and women acknowledge descent from a common totem, an ancestor perhaps partly human, partly animal: others claim kinship on the basis of one 'country', the track which one such ancestor followed in his wanderings: there are dream totemism, conception totemism, specially defined attitudes towards various natural species.

A person's totem is often described as his 'Dreaming', the literal translation of the term among some Aboriginal tribes. Even before his birth it is part of himself: and he in his turn, among many groups, may transmit it to his children. It is the essence of his spiritual past, a link with his ancestors who lived in what is known as the 'Eternal Dreamtime'. The great Beings of this period, who created not only the Aborigines themselves but their whole social order as well, are thought to be spiritually alive today just as much as they were in the past, and will be in the future.

But totemism itself is not religion. Fundamental as it is, it finds expression in religious doctrine and ceremony, in sacred mythology and song, just as it does in social relationships, and patterns of human behaviour.

To understand Aboriginal religion we must go further than this. We must examine its three-fold aspects—sacred ritual, sacred mythology, sacred song: for ritual enshrines and reflects mythology, expressed often through songs, and mythology in turn sanctions and gives meaning to ritual. Born into a society where faith and belief in established doctrines are taken for granted, rarely questioned, the Aborigines in their own life show a unity of interest and purpose which in itself reinforces their emotional fervour. Religion, among them, does not merely link man with the supernatural: it is a bond, too, uniting man with man in the consciousness of shared emotion, which reaches out from the past into the future--influencing his whole attitude to the process of living.

Let us glance for a moment at one part of the Continent —north-east and north-central Arnhem Land. Here, as elsewhere in Australia, the Aborigines are hunters and food-gatherers who depend on their environment for their very existence. The rhythm of the seasons, the growth of plants and food-bearing trees, the increase of animals, reptiles, birds and fish—upon these fundamental needs they have built up the framework of their religion, personalized and set in a human context by the great Ancestral Beings who created all life, and established all forms of behaviour.

The Djanggawul Brother and Sisters, most important of them all, coming out of the sunrise in their bark canoe: the two young Wauwalak Sisters: Laintjung, his face white with foam from the sea, and his son Banaitja: the light-skinned Baijini folk—these are some of the brilliant

figures who move across the mythological scene. They
introduced sacred ritual associated with their names, and
the sacred songs which commemorate their adventures;
and in them is the power, the force, which controls the
growth of living creatures and plants. To release this
force, the Aborigines must perform the appropriate
rituals, ensuring universal fertility. But the main theme
is the increase of human beings, the continuity of the
clan and the tribe: and all other features are merely
subsidiary. So we have here the stress on procreation, on
the importance of pregnancy and child-birth, and the
essential sequence of intercourse and conception, expressed over and over again in ritual and song.

There are other great fertility cults in Aboriginal
Australia, often diffused over immense areas. The Kunapipi, for instance, is still being carried from tribe to tribe
with glowing missionary zeal. Spread over hundreds of
miles, it is known by various alternate names; and
although its rituals and doctrine may not be the same
everywhere, its fundamental intent remains unchanged.
The name Kunapipi is of dual significance. On the one
hand it refers to a Fertility Mother, or Mothers, on the
other to the great Rainbow Snake who appears in various
guises all over Australia; and the stress placed upon
either depends on the tribe concerned.

Some people, in the religious cults which express their
deepest convictions, emphasize the male element at the
expense of the female: various tribes in New South Wales,
with their widespread Baiami cult, in the Great Victoria
Desert, and in Central Australia.

Nevertheless, belief in a Creative Mother, whatever
her name or mythology, is fundamental in Aboriginal
religion over much of the Continent. In western Arnhem
Land, the Mother is the inspiration and sponsor of the
great *ubar* cult. The Bathurst and Melville Islanders have

their Earth Mothers; so did the almost extinct Laragia who once owned the country about Darwin, the Daly River people, and those of the 'Buffalo' plains to the west of Oenpelli. The same cult spreads south and west, reaching the Tanami-Granites 'desert', and the Billaluna country in Western Australia.

In single or dual form, she is the living essence and symbol of fertility. From her, in the beginning, came all human beings and natural resources—and not the Aborigines alone, but people of every colour and race. Totemism and ritual stem from her; and through her intervention the Aboriginal Way can continue to function. She is 'our mother', sometimes cruel or harsh to the eyes of the stranger, but always deeply concerned with the well-being, the eternal renewal, of her Aboriginal devotees.

Often her aura is extended to embrace her counterparts, Aboriginal women—especially where much of the ritual centres about the increase and birth of human beings, women's special prerogative.

Men's more spectacular rôle, their greater activity in the religious as in the economic sphere, so impressed many early observers that they failed to perceive the fundamental balance which lay behind this division of labour. Women have their own share of ritual and song, sometimes their own ceremonies which no man may see. They know the mythological background, join in the special ritual tabus, gather food for the men who must do so much of the hard work. Even when their rôle seems insignificant to us, it is of vital importance to the success of the whole: for the men's more elaborate dances and decorations would be a failure without the women's active co-operation. Where women lose their interest in the sacred ceremonies of their tribe, turning their attention more and more to the ways of the white man, the

69

ritual structure is on the verge of collapse.

Sacred ritual is performed for the benefit of everyone in the group, not for the men alone, nor the women alone. Both must co-operate, in the fashion laid down by tradition: for here, as in all other aspects of life, their behaviour is complementary.

Aboriginal man feels himself to be in need of divine intervention, which will ensure his material and spiritual continuation. Without this, he could not cope with the exigencies of everyday existence. With it, his faith constantly renewed by sacred ritual, he is contented and safe, sure of his place in the universe, oriented to his satisfaction in space and time.

Widow's mourning ring from Bathurst Island.

CHAPTER X

Symbolism in Religion

ABSTRACT emotion is not easy to grasp or sustain. Human beings, it seems, can conceive of it only through material forms, in terms of their own experience. So religious faith, among the Aborigines, does not exist in a vacuum. It finds expression through words, through mental images based on concrete experience, through ritual and everyday behaviour, through song and chant, through material objects and emblems.

These symbols—the word, the action, the song, the emblem—are the outward expressions of inner sacred life. They are focal points, imbued with special significance, setting up a special train of thought in the minds of the listener or the beholder. Each has its meaning, or cluster of meanings—not always the same, for neophyte, novice, or uninitiated may view it with different eyes: but all, alike, conventionally determined. Each symbol serves as one key to the underlying background of belief, while a series of symbols may express in outline the religious ideology.

But such symbols are useless by themselves, divorced from their own setting. They retain their meaning only when people accept them as a part of normal life, as dynamic expressions of a still virile faith. Of course, there are archaic symbols which exist apart from their doctrinal background, unsubstantiated by myth or 'divine' explanation. But they cannot exist for long in their material expression, apart from their spiritual meaning. Symbols for symbolism's sake are not assured of survival; they will soon disappear, become attached to another symbol, or be imbued with a new meaning.

To the people within whose way of life they belong, they are meaningful and important: but outside the cultural context they may have a different meaning, or none at all. Thus the cross, as a symbol of Christianity, would mean nothing to an Australian Aboriginal totemite without Mission contact.

Symbols help Aboriginal man to develop and rein-vigorate his belief, explaining and substantiating religious ideology. The myth is translated, so to speak, by actual evidence which crystallizes his faith. 'This is how the Divine Being looked'. 'This his genital organ'. 'This his blood, and this his sacred stick', and so on.

The postulant in front of his ceremonial emblems feels himself very close to the 'divine' presence, to the Ancestral Being associated with them. The religious symbol is something very sacred. It is personalized, because its roots are firmly set in the mythological doctrine; it has meaning, and it emanates power.

Its importance as a visual aid to religious belief cannot be under-estimated. To the beholder, it means inspiration, emotional exhilaration, and a renewed belief in his own way of life.

In the big sacred rituals of Aboriginal Australia, postulants carry out special actions and dances. Away from

72

31. In the shelter of a windbreak, a woman mends a wooden dish with spinifex gum. A rough dish is beside the fire, and a child amuses himself with a mountain devil (lizard) that is resting on his head. Western Desert.   *Photograph: courtesy B. Tonkinson*

32. Girls begin to practise food collecting at quite an early age. A girl holds a wooden dish, near Jalara Soak, Western Desert.
Photograph: courtesy B. Tonkinson

33. A Desert family sets out for another waterhole. Western Desert.
Photograph: courtesy B. Tonkinson

34. Women and children using digging sticks to find yams. Haast's
Bluff, Central Australia, 1942.
Photograph: courtesy C. P. Mountford

Above: 35. Winnowing grass seed. Alkungunga, Mann Range, Central Australia, 1940.
Photograph: courtesy C. P. Mountford

Left: 36. Woman grinding grass seeds; her daughter plays alongside her. The flour accumulates in the dish. Gibson Desert, 1964-65.
Photograph: courtesy B. Tonkinson

Above : 37. Filling a dish with water from a rockhole Musgrave Ranges, 1940.
Photograph : courtesy C. P. Mountfor

Left : 38. Straightening a hunting spear. Ernabella, northern South Australia, 1940.
Photograph : courtesy C. P. Mountford

the general camp there is a sacred ground, round, oblong or variously shaped, and on it a hut or shelter in which may be stored sacred emblems.

During the rituals, actors perform symbolic actions relating to the Ancestral or Spirit Beings who sponsored the cult. As they dance and posture, others are singing—chanting, in outline, the cult's religious doctrine. The phrases they use are often symbolic, or create word pictures which mean various things to members of different age-groups attending the ceremonies.

In the course of the ceremony, the sacred objects are taken from their hiding place—the material symbols which validate the cult's mythology, through which is expressed the religious doctrine.

They vary considerably from tribe to tribe, ranging from naturalistic representations to others extremely stylized. Among them are wooden poles or figures beautifully decorated in ochres, hung with feathered pendants; long boards incised with designs; bullroarers to be twirled at the end of a length of twine; or emblems made from bound grass and paperbark, tied with human hair cord or fibres. In some of the women's secret ceremonies there are long painted poles, usually kept hidden away from men and children, and sometimes of phallic significance. But none of these objects are merely symbols; as the ritual progresses they become imbued with a power which is communicated to all participants.

The Aborigines of the Great Victoria (or Western) Desert number among their most sacred treasures several objects which, they believe, are metamorphosed Ancestral Beings. One is a dark green hand-polished stone said to be the body of Milbali, the white goanna, and another the body of Jungga, the black goanna. A stone dish is another Milbali woman; and carefully smeared with red ochre is a dessicated female body, now rather badly damaged by constant handling. These sacred objects and others like them are said to be 'law'; for the Ancestral Beings left them here on earth so that people should believe in their existence, and behave in accordance with the dictates of tradition. For years they have been carried down and around the Desert in anti-clockwise fashion from west to east, along a specified route; and on one occasion some of them even travelled as far as Broome, on the north-west coast. As soon as they arrive at a camp they are hurried into the bush and hidden away in a sacred storehouse, and there they serve as the focal point for several types of sacred ritual.

The passing on from camp to camp of these sacred relics, visible and tangible 'proof' which it is unthinkable that anybody should doubt, helps to keep alive men's faith in the spiritual reality which they substantiate. By contemplating and meditating upon them, as well as by taking part in the ceremonies associated with them, the initiate may come into direct contact with the Ancestral Beings and from them receive reassurance and strength.

To the casual stranger these objects may seem unimportant and even drab. How can a stone, however beautifully polished, or a partly broken human body, inspire such reverence? The answer, of course, lies in the emotional attitude of the beholder. The initiate 'knows' that this is no mere stone, but the material substance of a Being with whom he, himself, has a compelling spiritual relationship. His belief endows the stone with qualities which distinguish it from all other stones: and by the reverse process, the special nature of this stone reinforces his original convictions.

Let us consider an emblem from north-eastern Arnhem Land, signifying a goanna's tail and verterbrae. Totemic designs are painted down its trunk, and feathered pendants attached. Slowly the actor removes it from its shade, posturing as he does so; he writhes along the ground, holding the sacred stick close to his breast. Singing continues; he is revealing one of the mysteries to participant-onlookers, all highly-initiated men.

What does this mean? Here is an emblem which is a symbol of a goanna's tail and verterbrae, withdrawn from its shade. But to the neophyte it is much more than this. The shade or hut symbolizes a special conically-shaped mat, brought by the Djanggawul Fertility Mothers from a spirit land away in the sunrise, beyond the Morning Star. This mat is really a womb. When the goanna tail emblem is removed from it on the sacred ground, this signifies that the first people, ancestors of the present-day eastern Arnhem Landers, are being born from their Mother; and they, in turn, are associated with a combination of fertility symbols. Actually, there is symbol within symbol, meaning within meaning, much of it connected with fundamental drives.

These symbols do not stand alone as focal points, representations of mythological high-lights; nor are they used only to bring about one desired event. And they do not remain segregated symbols, relevant to sacred life alone. In varying degrees, they have a bearing on each and every aspect of Aboriginal life.

CHAPTER XI

Mythology

HOW can a non-literate people preserve its traditions, the knowledge which it considers relevant and important to everyday life? Only through word of mouth, transmitted from one generation to another. A gap in the process, a lapse of three or four generations, and the information is lost—or distorted beyond recognition.

Even without such interruptions, the substance of this verbal literature must have been changing slowly over the passing years—not only in detail, but in emphasis and interpretation. This can hardly be avoided. Even the presence of material symbols is only a partial check, because these, too, are dependent on verbal explanations.

What is more, especially in regard to mythology, no two storytellers will use exactly the same words. There are a few exceptions, where the actual words are handed down as part of the myth itself and supposed to be unalterable. But on the whole, given the essential framework, each storyteller will have a slightly different version, influenced by the points which have most interested him personally.

Between sacred and secular mythology there is no definite borderline.

Sacred myths are directly related to the religious life, and often their main features are acted out in sacred ritual. Mostly they concern the origin of the world, or the tribal country, of human beings and natural species. The wanderings of the great Ancestral Beings are enshrined in them, their deeds and adventures, even their very words. There are explanations of natural features, land and sea, sun, moon and stars: of ritual and ceremony, and of ordinary patterns of social behaviour. All have some bearing on the life and well-being of the people to whom they belong.

Again, there are differences between one group of tribes and another. In New South Wales there were the myths of Daramulan and Baiami, Sky Heroes, responsible for instituting sacred ritual. In south-eastern South Australia there were Nurunderi, Nepeli, and others, responsible for creating physical features like the Murray River. Through the Dieri country, around Lake Eyre and Coopers Creek, were the many *muramura* Ancestral Spirits, like Darana, the Creator of the first human beings, or the Gadimagara, part-human part-gigantic goanna (or 'crocodile').

Darana was the most powerful of the *muramura,* and the first one to come out of the earth: he controlled the sky and the winds, and could cause droughts or make rain at his pleasure. Once, after a heavy shower, great numbers of witchetty grubs appeared in the ground. Darana gathered them by singing one of his songs, then dried them and collected them in string bags which he hung on a tree. When his two sons, the Daraulu, came up and saw the bags hanging there, they mischievously threw their boomerangs at them: and one struck a bag, tearing a great hole. Dust came pouring out and blew everywhere, in far-reaching clouds of dust which darkened the sun and caused a terrible drought. All the people were starving, and the tribesmen were desperate. The other *muramura,* when they learned what the Daraulu youths had done, angrily strangled and killed them: but Darana magically brought them back to life. Then the *muramura* killed them again, and rolled up their bodies to form two egg-shaped objects which for generations the Dieri people kept as sacred emblems.

In other stories men turn into birds, lizards, spiders, sometimes having the power to resume human shape when they wish.

Over the Great Victoria Desert from north to south, from east to west, roamed the two Goanna Men, the Wadi Gudjara, totemic in essence—wandering across the red sand and the spinifex country from waterhole to soak, creating, meeting other Beings, performing sacred ritual. They came in contact with the powerful dual Spirit called Njirana-Julana, with the Opossum Woman, the Moon Man, and the woman who was the ancestral Mountain Devil.

There is the Minma Didi, a small brown bird, once an old woman who used to collect snakes in a skin bag. Finally the bag became too full, and burst, so that all the snakes fell out. Didi ran away: but where the bag fell a clay-pan was formed, while the snakes were metamorphosed into stones. This place is now an increase site.

Throughout the country these Beings journeyed, leaving a maze of tracks, dotted with sacred sites where they rested, or performed special acts. Some have changed into stone, and can still be seen to-day—like Tor Rock, on the north-west Arnhem Land coast, who came with his family at the beginning of time from the islands of Indonesia. Others live on only in spirit form, or have found material expression in various birds and animals, insects and reptiles.

On the eastern corner of Arnhem Land, the Djanggawul Brother and Sisters came out of the sea on the path of the Morning Star from the Sun, their Mother. Overland and among the adjacent islands they travelled across to the west, into the setting sun; and on their way they gave birth to the first people, and introduced sacred ritual. Laintjung too came out of the sea at Blue Mud Bay, his face stained with foam; and though he was fiinally put to death his son Banaitja, the Barramundi, survived to carry on his ritual and doctrine. On a lonely stretch of coastline Rabaraba wanders forever collecting oysters and shellfish, while her husband Karmali paddles his canoe among the islands in search of fish. Kultana and his wife live among the wild rice and the mangroves at 'Badu' or Mudilnga, home of some of the Arnhem Land dead, sending the cold winds and rain to the living. Wudal or Woijal, of the boomerang legs, whose name is linked with wild honey and gum tree blossoms, came northwards long ago through the dry gorges and scrub of the inland. And the Wauwalak Sisters came up to the coast from the South, to be finally swallowed by the immense Rock Python or Rainbow Snake at Muruwul waterhole.

There is Kunapipi, or Kalwadi, with her far-flung cult among tribes who speak different languages, but know the key words and songs associated with her rituals; and in the west of Arnhem Land there is the creative Mother Waramurunggoindju, who came out of the sea from 'Macassar' to land on the Australian mainland. It was she, together with the famous Jurawadpad,[8] who inspired the sacred *ubar* rituals.

According to some versions Jurawadpad was her first husband: but all agree that he was old and bald when he married, against her will, a young girl named Minaliwul. She rejected all his advances—crying when he approached her, refusing the choice foods that he brought to please her. Night and day she thought only of her young lover Bulugu, the water snake. At last Jurawadpad discovered the truth, and in a rage he planned his revenge. Out in the bush he made an *ubar*, a special hollow log: then back to the camp he went with the news that hunting fires had been lit in the Bush, and now was the time to catch goanna and bandicoot. Minaliwul and her mother set off together: but Jurawadpad went quickly ahead by another track to the hollow log, and crawling inside turned into a snake. He summoned a host of birds to circle near him, attracting the two women from far away so that they hurried to see what animals might be there. First Minaliwul probed inside the log with a stick: then she inserted her hand, and at once the snake struck. It attacked her mother as well, and when both lay dead Jurawadpad came out again in the shape of a man. Today he is a venomous snake, said to be specially dangerous to young girls of Minaliwul's age: and his hollow log is the modern *ubar,* the centre of sacred ritual. Like many myths his story contains a wealth of details: yet its importance lies not in the bare outline, but in the symbolism which it offers to the initiated.

Great and powerful Beings of varying ritual significance are everywhere in Aboriginal mythology. The Wondjina of the Kimberleys: the Djundagal Python of western-central Northern Territory: the Wonambi Rainbow Snake of northern South Australia: the fascinating fair-haired Mungamunga girls, swaying their buttocks as they pass across desert and plain, singing their songs and manipulating sacred emblems: the powerful Eaglehawk of the Roper River who killed Mumuna, the Great Mother: Wuratilagu, the Spirit Woman of Groote Eylandt, who

39. A hunter returns with his catch, followed by his dog. Mt. Conner, Central Australia, 1940.
Photograph : courtesy C. P. Mountford

40. A hunter with a cat he has killed. Ayers Rock, Central Australia, 1940.
Photograph : courtesy C. P. Mountford

41. Mother and child asleep. Musgrave Ranges, 1940.
Photograph: courtesy C. P. Mountford

42. Baby asleep in a wooden dish. Haast's Bluff, Central Australia, 1942.
Photograph: courtesy C. P. Mountford

43. Paintings on rock in front of the well-known Lightning Brothers (which were illustrated in *Australian Aboriginal Art*.) This site is associated with rain making. Delamere, Northern Territory.
Photograph : courtesy E. J. Brandl

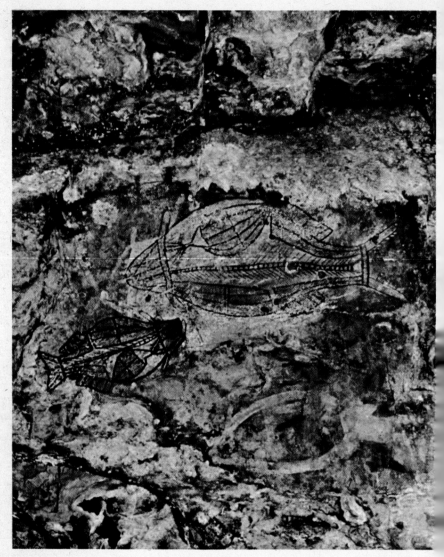

44. Typical X-ray paintings of fish, in a cave near Mount Brockman,
Northern Territory; the central fish is 51 cm long.
Photograph: courtesy E. J. Brandl

decided that females should be partially segregated from their menfolk, and hid herself from the eyes of prying men beneath a covering of bark: or Nimparipari of Bathurst and Melville Islands, manifesting himself as a shooting star.

Some of these myths are known only to initiated men: but more often all the adults in a community, and even children in many cases, are acquainted at least with their outline. The difference lies in the details, in their symbolism, or esoteric significance: for these may not be revealed to everyone, and frequently they are closely linked with various stages of sacred ritual.

Secular myths, in contrast, have little or no religious or ritual significance. They are told for enjoyment and entertainment as people gather about the campfires, old men and women perhaps taking turns in recounting stories learnt in childhood or youth.

Their range of subjects is wide. Some are tales with a moral, pointing out the retribution that follows anti-social behaviour. Some describe the creation of natural features by minor Ancestral Beings—the making of small hills, or rocks, or patches of bush and jungle. Others explain the peculiarities of various creatures the Aborigines come upon in the course of their daily routine: how the echidna or porcupine got his quills: how the emu became a bird: how the blanket lizard developed his frill. Many of these, indeed, have some trace of sacredness.

Then there are stories of spirit beings, malignant and otherwise—giants who captured and ate human beings in mythological times, or contemporary spirits of one kind and another who may still be encountered today. Spiirts of the dead, visiting their living kin: meteor spirits, violent and unpredictable: quiet spirits, friendly to man.

There is the lonely crocodile who kidnapped a young

girl and took her to wife, only to suffer for his audacity: the man who could not resist making sweethearts among women forbidden to him by tribal law: the stone flint lying among the sand-dunes, a man-eating spirit in disguise: the man who committed incest with his daughter, but came to an unhappy end. Or the widely distributed story of Nori the owl, and his uncle Kakala the white cockatoo. Kakala cunningly attracted two young girls, Mararu the bandicoot, and Windari a short tailed marsupial, by making himself look pretty: while Nori was ugly like a piece of wood. Later Nori stole his uncle's feathers and ornaments, and shut him up in a cave: then he took possession of the two women, who accepted him happily now that his personal appearance was changed. But his pleasure was short-lived, for Kakala escaped and soon had them back again in his keeping.

We hear of Tulina the giant, married to one of the *mamu* spirit people whom he fought till they finally killed him: of the lonely traveller, terrified by the dead man he encounters at dusk: of the young brother who loved his sister, and met with a violent death: of Pomapoma the trickster, with his brazen defiance of tribal convention: and of the Turtle Woman, fatal to human beings who catch a glimpse of her, living alone under the seas of her home, which men call Poison Island.

The story-teller uses vivid gestures and changes of tone, leaping suddenly to his feet or collapsing dramatically to the ground while his audience sits entranced. Sometimes, in places like Oenpelli, he illustrates special points by painting them on the walls of a cave, or on pieces of stringy-bark; or he draws his pictures only in shifting sand, to disappear perhaps even while he is speaking.

Mythology, sacred or secular or in-between, is the basis upon which Aboriginal life is constructed. In it, coming down out of the past, are all the experience and traditions which have accumulated over the ages—the verbal literature which expresses, in frank or symbolic form, the essence of the Aboriginal Way.

Postulants dancing during a Kalwadi (Fertility Mother) ceremony; crayon drawing, from Birrundudu, Northern Territory.

CHAPTER XII

Ritual and Ceremony

THE past brought to life again in the present, the present projected into the future—this, in effect, is sacred ceremony. Re-enactment of mythological scenes is no mere play-acting, no dramatic device to fill in an idle hour. The men and women who practise it do so in deadly earnest, convinced that on the success of their effort depends their own welfare and that of their neighbours. It is a serious matter, with no half measures: for the sceptic and the dissenter, found only today among those whose faith has been shaken by the introduction of alien values, no longer participate in these sacred rites.

Some of the ceremonies are performed by men alone, on their sacred dancing ground where none but the initiated may come. Others are only for women, away from the main camp out of sight of their menfolk. And in some both men and women participate, each sex with its clearly defined rôles.

There are ceremonies which, for all their significance, seem to the outsider dull and rather monotonous; others so vivid and breath-taking that spectator as well as dancer is lost in the spell.

In one area there may be only one main series of rituals: in another several series of equal importance. A sacred ceremony may be more or less a local affair: or it may involve hundreds of people who come for many miles to gather at some pre-arranged site. Small hunting bands which have been scattered across the 'deserts' come together again for seasonal ceremonies, as the tribes about Ooldea do at the first new moon of Spring. Friends and relatives greet one another with happy tears after months of separation, and under the shadow of the sacred rituals betrothals are arranged or confirmed, goods are exchanged, and grievances settled—if possible, without bloodshed. Ideally, quarrelling should not be allowed to disrupt the sacred ceremonies: but sometimes, in this highly charged atmosphere, sharp words lead to blows and spearings. The trouble spreads until, split by opposing factions, the whole gathering breaks up in confusion.

Whatever ill-feeling is present, it should not be shown on the sacred ground. In the main camp this is less imperative, but during the rituals themselves control is strict. The participants should submerge their personal identity, entering so wholeheartedly into the ceremonies that through their actions present and past become one.

In these sacred rituals man comes into direct contact with the spiritual forces which, he believes, control the world as he knows it. Perhaps, if left to themselves, they would continue to attend to his well-being, and maintain the *status quo*: but he cannot leave this to chance. Only by keeping in touch with them, by re-enacting their travels and re-affirming their edicts, can he feel sure of his own place in the world.

Nearly everywhere in Aboriginal Australia, most of the

85

principal religious ceremonies have a common basic intent, springing from two of the fundamental drives of man—hunger and sex. To survive, men must have food, as the Aborigines with their direct dependence on nature are well aware: and the striking phenomena of birth and death, however constantly repeated, seem to have left their mark in Aboriginal myth and ceremony. These vital ingredients are treated sometimes crudely, sometimes subtly, sometimes veiled by a colourful and delicate web of symbolism and imagery. But in greater or lesser degree they are always present, lending urgency and reality to the dramatic ritual woven around them.

Throughout the Continent increase ceremonies and rites have been reported, centring about the growth and renewal of vegetable and animal foods: yams or lily roots, kangaroos, snakes, birds or small marsupials. Some of them are slight and almost mechanical, with the minimum of elaboration. Others again give rise to brilliant tableaux like those which marked the goose-egg festival of the old Daly River tribes. At the end of the rainy season, wild geese nest in their thousands among the swamps and billabongs of the low lying green plains. Then the canoes would go paddling down the waterways, to return laden with eggs, as people gathered for the great *karamala* ceremonies when young boys were initiated. Under the tall trees by the river bank, as steam rose from the earth ovens, the boys were heaped high with warm goose eggs until only their heads showed: and later in careful dancing and mimicry the life cycle of the goose was enacted before them.

At Melville and Bathurst Islands, where the Sun Mother was held in veneration, the most important event of the whole year was the ceremonial series for the increase of the *kulama* yams. Boys and girls, faces painted in the startling patterns characteristic of these islands, went through various stages of their initiation into adult life with no more alarming physical operation than the pulling out of facial and body hair: and both men and women joined equally in the festivities. None of the songs at such a time were traditional. Novices and older participants alike produced their own compositions based on personal experience, accompanied by actions and dancing: 'The whirlwind is shaking the leaves from the trees, and blowing them upwards', one singer declaimed. 'I saw two sharks fighting', another began his song: and a third, 'There's nobody now at Munubi, only flies . . .' Many of the most spirited or appealing songs and the names of their singers are remembered for years, although the *kulama* festivals themselves have now all but collapsed.

Imagine, now, a brief scene from Central Australia, as we stand with a group of men in a sandy clearing among the scrub. First a Euro dancer comes leaping across the ground, scratching himself, peering about him, and nibbling from time to time at a special ball that he carries. Then a Kangaroo and a species of Night Bird dance on to the ground, dramatizing part of a myth relating to circumcision. The novices in a corner beside their guardians raise their heads to look: but as each dancer makes to jump on them they are turned quickly over again on to their faces. Then an actor lavishly decorated with ochres and feather down comes out from among the bushes, holding behind him a sacred *wonigi* emblem. He advances deliberately, lifting his knees high and alighting almost on tip toe: and at every few paces, while the novices watch he inserts the *wonigi* pole into the ground before him. Finally, with a sudden shout, he plunges the pole directly in front of the novices, and as their guardians instantly turn them over he disappears towards the sacred storehouse to hide it.

Or take a scene from the widespread *kunapipi* rituals.

87

Two older men appear on the dancing ground, wearing tall conical headdresses. A pad of grass or bark is bound tightly with human hair twine so that it tapers up to a point: upon this feather down is fastened with blood in a curving snake design, and at the apex is a bunch of white cockatoo feathers. The headdress itself is a pandanus (a screw palm), and sways in the dance just as the pandanus foliage moves with the swell of the water. Two huge *jelmalandji* emblems, bearing the same arresting snake design, stand by a crescent-shaped trench where the novices wait. The two actors come dancing forward. They kneel beneath the *jelmalandji*, the leader singing and clapping his sticks as all the men surge round them. They shake their headdresses, loosening them until the leader knocks them easily to the ground. Then he rubs himself against the actors, to become spiritually one with them. The novices, too, and strangers not fully acquainted with *kunapipi* ritual, are rubbed against the headdresses or the down on the actors' bodies: this contact transfers 'power' from one to the other. Then the sacred invocations are called over the actors, as they shake themselves ritually, to the accompaniment of the beating sticks.

In western Arnhem Land the *ubar* rituals are perhaps the oldest, and still the most important: but through the influence of tribes to the east and south-east other ceremonies have been steadily gaining ground. To explain this, the western Arnhem Landers fall back on the myth of Lumaluma, the whale.

Long ago, Lumaluma was a man. He travelled along the coast from eastern Arnhem Land, singing and dancing: and as he came he seized all the best yams and foods, declaring them sacred to himself. The people grumbled at this, but took no action until he began to eat men, women, and children in all the camps through which he passed. Then they surrounded him, throwing their spears

45. X-ray painting of fish, 91 cm long: other blurred designs surround it. In a rock shelter between the East Alligator River and Red Lily Lagoon, Northern Territory.
Photograph: courtesy E. J. Brandl

46. X-ray fish painting, 127 cm long, surrounded by other designs, most notably red-ochre human figures and hand stencils (upper left-hand side). Djerlandjal Rock, near Mt. Brockman, Northern Territory.
Photograph: courtesy E. J. Brandl

47. The central figure of a hunter (X-ray type) holds a spear in a thrower in one hand and a goose-wing fan in the other, along with spears. From his neck hangs a dilly bag. Length of the figure from peg of spearthrower to foot at right is approximately 142 cm. Human and other figures surround him, superimposed on other designs of a complex nature. Djerlandjal Rock, near Mt. Brockman, Northern Territory.

Photograph : courtesy E. J. Brandl

48. A hunter lies asleep, his spears and thrower beside him. This figure, about 76 cm long, is superimposed on a complex sorcery painting of a woman: the conventionalized drawing is distorted, as is usual in figures of this variety. Beneath this again is a large X-ray fish—probably a barramundi, as this is a barramundi increase site. The fish is superimposed on earlier unidentified drawings. Other figures surround these. The meanings were supplied by two Maiali men, Namandjalawogwog and Djimungur. Djerlandjal Rock, near Mt. Brockman, Northern Territory.

Photograph: courtesy E. J. Brandl

until he lay wounded on the beach: but as they were about to deal him the final blow he spoke. 'Don't kill me yet,' he pleaded. 'Let me show you my ceremonies before I die!' So they held their spears, and waited. He showed them the *mareiin*, the sacred rituals from eastern Arnhem Land associated there with the Djanggawul cult. Then he showed them the *ubar*, then the *djunggawon* or *lorgan*,[9] the *kunapipi* and the *djadbangari*, and a host of others. By the time he had finished the last ceremony, all the people were crying. 'Look at me now', he told them. 'I'm going far out to sea, where I won't trouble you again. But I've left you all my ceremonies. Now I'm no longer a man: I'm Lumaluma the whale!' Crying, they watched him rise out of the water, and saw a jet of water spurt from his wounded body. Lumaluma has never returned; but ever since that day the people of western Arnhem Land have been performing the ceremonies he brought them.

The importance of sacred ritual to the Aborigines themselves, the enthusiasm and unity of purpose with which they perform it, overshadow their genuine interest in rituals of a more secular kind. But these, although they lack the solemnity and the driving force of the others, seem in a sense equally necessary to their well-being. There are love magic rituals, for instance, some linked with the great fertility ceremonies, and others of a more mechanical kind—like the charming of a desired sweetheart's lock of hair. There are gay light-hearted dances which afford relaxation after a tiring or monotonous day, always to the accompaniment of singing and clapping sticks, or the drone of the didgeridoo. The actors are sea-birds, whirling and swooping; buffaloes stalked by a hunter; or (these days) aeroplanes gliding to land. These dances, as the Aborigines view them, are purely for pleasure, bringing them the exhilaration of rhythmic movement and song, and even at times taking the sharpness from an unhappy situation by allowing them to laugh, however briefly, at their troubles. The policeman, the cattle station man, the hard-bitten trader, are somehow less disturbing when they can be mimicked and joked about in the camps.

Sacred ceremonies come and go, in all their variety and complexity. There are times when for days or weeks everything is subordinated to the rituals out on the men's dancing ground, or the women's dancing ground, or about the main camp itself. Ritual calling, perhaps, goes on all night, with the women answering the cry of the men: the voice of the 'Mother', the *ubar* gong, echoes among the rocks without a pause till the ceremonies are done: people observe certain food tabus, submit to a series of body paintings, or spend night after night dancing and singing in relays. They may cleanse themselves ritually, as the northern Arnhem Landers do after the *mareiin* ceremonies—men, women and children rushing together into the water. They may throw themselves into the mortuary singing for a dead man or woman, or work themselves up to a high pitch of excitement when the young boys are initiated.

But these things do not happen every day. In the intervals between the big ceremonies, secular singing and dancing come into their own. Rhythmic action and music, planned with deliberate intent or a spontaneous gesture of enjoyment, are a part of true Aboriginal life. A camp without ceremonies, where moonlit evenings are silent, or broken only by the muttering of the card-players or a sudden burst of quarrelling, is a camp where the people's zest for living has been lost or diverted into other and less satisfying channels. Where sacred ritual has been allowed to lapse, people no longer maintain conscious contact with their own traditions and back-

90

ground: and once this vital link has been broken, the whole course of their lives must reflect the change.

A ceremony in progress; west-central Northern Territory.

CHAPTER XIII

Songs

A STILL night, with moonlight silver on the sand, and the lingering smell of sandalwood smoke from dozens of small fires: and filling the whole air, resonant and vibrating like the beat of a living heart, the clap, clap, clap of the beating sticks. Or the hypnotizing throb of the drone-pipe, echoing among the rocks or through the mangroves of tidal creeks and coastline. But above it all, above the regular stamp or shuffle of dancing feet, come the rise and fall of the singing.

Perhaps the rhythm is sharp and staccato: or a lilting tune sung with a full chorus of voices. The tones may be deep and clear, a cluster of men or a songman singing alone: the lighter sound of the women may drift from the distance, from one of their secret ceremonies: or the gay singing of young men, punctuated with shouts of applause, may continue far into the night.

Sometimes people sing in the daytime—men gathered for sacred rituals, women painting themselves with ochres ready for dancing, children enjoying the fun of their own songs. Or a woman wailing and sobbing, mourning the sickness or death of one of her close kin.

From the rhythm or tune alone, now and then, we can tell the theme of the singing—especially where the same songs and rhythms have spread across hundreds of miles. But as a rule we must know the words—sometimes in the language of the singers themselves, sometimes in an alien tongue belonging to tribes from whom they originally came.

Over most of Australia the songs are short—a few key words repeated over and over, with constant but insignificant changes. In contrast, those of north and north-eastern Arnhem Land are long and elaborate, building up detailed pictures, theme within theme.

Most vivid of all, perhaps, are the sacred songs, nearly always linked with ritual or dancing, with special symbols and emblems. A whole myth or series of myths may be told in song: or songs may be used to outline and imprint on the listeners' minds its most significant points. They are always traditional, altered only slightly (so we are told) over the centuries: for the words themselves, and not merely their contents, are sacred. Some of them may be heard or sung only by initiated men, others only by adult women: and others again by both, assembled together. Long cycles of songs may belong to different clans, or different totemic groups, or to special cults with their ceremonial headmen.

There are secular songs, too, merging at times into the sacred. Mourning songs, that tell of the spirit's wanderings among its kin, or in the land of the dead—like the appealing impromptu chants of Bathurst and Melville Islands, or the poetic Morning Star singing of northern Arnhem Land. Songs about spirits, about birds and animals, or the changing seasons. Or songs that catch the highlights of alien contact, often sharpened and clarified by shrewd mimicry, and lively dancing—songs of camels and Afghan traders, passed up through the 'desert' tribes to the Victoria River country, or of Chinese fishermen about Wyndham, carrying fish slung from poles over their shoulders: of white policemen coming into the camps, selecting young girls to take with them as 'witnesses', or of aeroplanes and R.A.A.F. camps in the Crocodile Islands of the Arnhem Land coast.

Some of these modern series belong to special songmen, who with the help of spirit or totemic familiars compose their own individual songs. In western Arnhem Land, for example, are the famous 'gossip song' cycles, relating local scandal and love affairs but cautiously failing to mention names.

Whatever the subject matter, the Aborigines find in song an outlet for their emotion, superficial or deep as the case may be. Sorrow and joy, anger and grief, vigorous pleasure in life and urge for rhythmic expression—all find utterance and release through stylized patterns of song, with their active complement of ritual and dance.

CHAPTER XIV

Artist and Craftsman

S ONGMAN and dancer, hunter and drone-pipe player, adolescent and grandparent—all must work with their hands, fashioning objects of use and beauty. Nothing is mass-produced. Working with simple tools, each man and woman finds individual expression in creating something to fulfil a definite need. Very few of their products are clumsy or crudely finished: children's toys, roughly modelled wax figures used in sorcery, a child's first efforts at basket-making or carving. But for the most part they take a pride in their work, and the finished specimen is a masterpiece of its kind.

Everyday objects like spear and spearthrower, club and boomerang, have a balance and line which their maker takes for granted; dillybags and baskets are carefully twined, sometimes painted, or patterned with stylized figures; an ordinary fighting stick may be beautified by the long curves of a yellow snake. Small wooden bobbins or spools for winding native string may be delicately incised, or painted with coloured ochres; and a plain wooden dish for carrying seeds and fruits has a smooth curve which makes it something more than an object of mere utility.

Forms and motifs are circumscribed in range, limited by locally accepted categories framed by tradition. Subject matter and style are not uniform throughout the Continent, despite some broad similarities. Just as different Aboriginal groups have their own versions of myth and ritual, so are there regional differences in their art. And within this context each person has his special approach —particularly in the field of sacred and ritual objects. Looking at ochre paintings on strips of bark, and knowing the artists, we can notice the individual touches that distinguish one from another.

There are paintings on rocks and caves, and on the human body: elaborate ground drawings, and wooden carvings. Some are realistic or natural, others so highly conventionalized that only those who know can explain their meaning. But none is devoid of significance. Many have ritual associations, or links with special stories and songs; and all are made with some purpose in view. Artistic merit is, in this sense, of minor importance: but the craftsman's content in his work, the artist's delight in a well-poised drawing, are no less real for being only partly deliberate.

Tribes of the Great Victoria Desert use long wooden boards in sacred ritual, incised with designs that symbolize the travels of Ancestral Beings. Waterholes too are shown, while conventional signs refer to incidents and to the actual bodies of the sacred Beings. Similar are the stone *tjurunga* of Central Australia, with their curving patterns of spiral and concentric circle so satisfying to the eye.

Further north we find the exotic paraphernalia of the Kunapipi fertility cult—tall ceremonial emblems of grass and paperbark built up on a central pole, made

49. Various red-ochre figures, some possibly drawn for sorcery. These are typical of the so-called Mimi (match-like spirit) art of western Arnhem Land. The full size of this mural is 2.4 m by 2.1 m. Rock shelter on top of a hill in the vicinity of Cahill's Crossing on the East Alligator River, Northern Territory.
Photograph: courtesy E. J. Brandl

50. Describing paintings in Initiation Cave at Ayers Rock, Central Australia, 1940. This site on the western side of the Rock was secret-sacred and associated with the mythic *Mala* (hare wallaby) : it is now a tourist attraction.
Photograph : courtesy C. P. Mountford

Above: 51. Cave paintings at Jessie Gap, Macdonnell Ranges, Central Australia. Formerly secret-sacred, these represent the mythic site of Witchetty Grubs.
Photograph: courtesy C. P. Mountford

Right: 52. An artist with his palette, painting on stringy-bark. Goulburn Island, western Arnhem Land, 1961.

Above : 53. An artist painting on stringybark. Elcho Island, north-eastern Arnhem Land, 1961.

Left : 54. A decorated *djuwei* post representing one of the mythic Wawalag Sisters and used in *djunggawon* rituals. The shredded bark is her hair, and the feathered pendant a chaplet she wears. The main post is her body, with ochred designs. The artist sits beside it. Elcho Island, 1964.

colourful by ochres and feather down, and pearl-shells to represent the eyes of the Mother. Then on the coast of Arnhem Land, more than anywhere else in Australia, the Aborigines have a wealth of material possessions, some rigidly conventionalized and others extremely naturalistic. Here, in fact, we have the art of a comparatively sophisticated people,[10] who through the centuries have been able to adjust themselves in some measure to alien infiltration. The semi-stylized carved human figures and heads, the graceful sacred objects and emblems, the complex bark paintings, all indicate a materially rich culture. Associated with this we find a society which has a structure elastic enough to permit of individual variations on traditional themes, and the energy to have developed through the ages its own characteristic 'school of art'.

Among the Kimberley rocks are the famous *wondjina* drawings, representing creative Beings of the Eternal Dreaming. And hundreds of miles east, in western Arnhem Land, realistic or stylized designs in coloured ochres and blood crowd the walls of the caves. The rock floors are polished and worn, by countless artists sitting or lying there over the centuries. Some of the drawings are high up on the face of sheer cliffs, sheltered by overhanging rocks, where the artists would have been forced to balance on crudely made ladders, or notched posts. Others are on the very roofs of caves, awkward even to look at: so it is hard to imagine how the artist had the patience to lie there, with neck strained, intent on his animated and graceful patterns.

Although there are other beautiful cave paintings throughout the Continent, these 'galleries' north and east of Oenpelli hold specimens almost unsurpassed in Aboriginal Australia: grotesque figures of human beings, with bird, reptile or animal features; Rainbow Snakes;

x-ray drawings of creatures and people, showing their bones and internal organs; 'match-stick' drawings of people or spirits called *mimi*, hunting or dancing. Some of them are drawn there for special reasons, religious or magical, for increase or sorcery; and often there are long stories about them. Old drawings may be retouched, or obliterated to make way for new ones: but on some walls succeeding generations of artists have simply superimposed their own, making at first glance a complex jumble of outline and colour.

Then there are the wooden mortuary posts of Bathurst and Melville Islands—no two alike, all strikingly coloured and carved; the wooden human figures of north-east Arnhem Land; elaborate headdresses and emblems, often hung with yards of rosy parakeet feathers; special dancing masks of Cape York Peninsula; baskets of painted stringy-bark, and conical grass mats; conventional wooden birds and animals, used in ritual; hollow wooden drums or gongs, from which comes the voice of the great Fertility Mother.

Many of these, no matter how many hours of loving care has gone into their making, are not expected to last. Once the ritual is over they are dismantled, or thrown away—cast into a sacred waterhole, or left to decay. When the need arises again people will make new ones, singing or chanting as they chip away at the wood, or work in the feathers. Bush fires sweep through the scrub, razing the massive grave posts: and termites and borers complete the work of destruction.

But the stone *tjurunga* of Central Australia, like the painted stones of western Arnhem Land, are used and treasured by generations of tribesmen. The precious wooden boards of the desert are carefully ochred and greased, kept on racks within special shelters: and the hard wooden poles, the sacred drone-pipes and drums (or gongs) of Arnhem Land, are preserved for years. Cave walls in various parts of Australia hold paintings of which, perhaps, no living man or woman can tell the meaning. And the rock carvings of New South Wales and Victoria have long survived the passing of the people to whom they were no fantastic relic, but a living and significant part of everyday life.

In the changing scene of to-day, as the native population dwindles and tradition steadily loses its force and meaning, a new kind of Aboriginal artist has made his appearance. To many people who gave no thought to Aboriginal art, ignoring or even denying its presence among them, the name of Albert Namatjira is a household word. The Central Australian artists of the Hermansburg school—the Namatjiras, the Pareroultjas, Ebatarinja, Raberaba and Moketarinja—using European techniques and tools, have captured the imagination of the Australian city-dweller as no purely indigenous artist has been able to do.

The tribesman working patiently with his familiar ochres and brushes, his canvas of bark or rock, his incising tools of stone or (these days) of steel, has no interest in achieving recognition beyond his own immediate circle. He knows, as he paints a 'clan' design on his neighbour's chest, that his subject will compensate him for his trouble: but beyond this he is not concerned with commercializing his art. Perhaps as the old incentives decline, and new distractions occupy his attention, the artist may not only lose the pleasure he once took in his work, but find no occasion to practise his craft at all. Then, as has happened in so many parts of the Continent, what survives of Aboriginal art in that area may be relegated to museum study—however interesting, however aesthetically pleasing, it is no longer living art, no longer personally significant to any contemporary group of people. Perhaps, on the other hand, the artist may do as Namatjira and his colleagues have done. He may learn to employ new tools, in a different way, adopting a different approach to his subject, and developing his talent in this new direction not only for his own gratification but also as a means of achieving material reward. Then his work, beautiful or exciting as it may be, cannot be called predominantly Aboriginal in inspiration or context: for the artist alone is of Aboriginal birth, his means of expression pre-eminently European. Or perhaps, though the artist him-self must accept change in a changing world, he need not resort to either of these extremes. Perhaps with these new techniques and new means of expression he can combine the inspired skill of the true Aboriginal crafts-man, delving into the rich heritage of Aboriginal lore and translating it proudly and vividly in terms which all can read.

X-ray drawing of kangaroo and hunter; from Oenpelli cave painting.

CHAPTER XV

Law and Order

OUR Continent is wide, with its vast inland of plain and 'desert': for many years the difficulties of communication baffled even the white man's skill. It is little wonder, then, that the loosely organized tribes had no central governing body, and failed to unite against the white invader. Loyalty was something localized, confined to the land and the people they knew. Strangers, Aboriginal or not, were on an entirely different basis: for barriers of distrust and suspicion separated tribe from tribe, relaxed only when trading or sacred ceremonies brought neighbours together on friendly terms.

Consciousness of a shared tradition, of ritual and sacred mythology held in common, has served to widen the tribal horizon, bringing more people into the safe, known world of human beings. Quarrels, or bitter fighting, might still continue: but they take place within the range of known behaviour, where the rules of killing or making peace were understood and accepted.

Not all mythology, sacred or secular, defines the patterns

of human conduct. But many Ancestral Beings are said to have laid down certain precepts, or made suggestions which human beings were expected to follow. They determined, broadly, the rôles of men and women in ritual and economic life, in bearing and raising children, in marriage, and at death. And they introduced tabus of various kinds, with penalties for infringement. Some of their warnings and suggestions are soundly based, and have been of value in adjusting the people to their environment. But this does not, of itself, ensure their acceptance. It is their supernatural origin which gives them force and significance as 'divine' decrees.

Thus within a tribe there are recognized codes of behaviour, sanctioned by tradition, and reinforced by the strong pressure of public opinion. In cases of doubt, decisions are made by the old people, and especially the old men who have shown themselves capable and vigorous exponents of their own way of life. Trivial offences committed by adults or children are handled by the immediate family or kin, but at formal initiation the tribe or the clan intervenes more directly in the discipline of the growing boy and girl.

From an early age, the child is conditioned to accept local standards of thought and behaviour. The issues are clear, not clouded by the necessity to make any serious choice: for the main course of life is already decided. Thus the child is prepared to conform, to believe that the code presented to him is not merely the best, but indeed the only possible one.

To strengthen this feeling, outlets are provided for harmful or destructive emotions which might cause trouble. Listening to various popular stories, for instance, people can enjoy the vicarious experience of breaking tabus, or acting in ways usually classed as wrong: but in the end conformity is encouraged, and the wrongdoer often, though not always, suffers for his misdeeds.

In ordinary life, rewards of one kind or another are offered for good behaviour. A man who fulfils his kinship obligations, who takes a keen interest in ceremony and tradition, who is an industrious and successful hunter, earns the approval of all his fellows—and may become a ceremonial headman as well.

On the other hand, ridicule is a powerful weapon for shaming people into compliance. So is the fear of sorcery, or of the supernatural punishment which may automatically follow the breach of some tabu, or marked carelessness in dancing, ritual or singing. Then there is the threat of physical violence, perhaps of death, for infringing some tribal or sacred law—or, more serious still, of being deprived of the usual mortuary rites. Nobody wants his body, or that of a close relative, to be thrown aside for the dogs and the crows to eat.

Aboriginal Australia has had, as a rule, no formal gatherings in the nature of law courts. Only the almost extinct Narrinyeri tribes at the mouth of the River Murray had organized meetings, in which old men and women always took the lead. In most cases, everyone is free to voice an opinion; talking and arguments may go on for weeks before any definite action is taken. But in serious ritual offences the main ceremonial leaders may decide on the punishment, and carry it out in secret, without consulting anyone else or describing what they have done.

Deliberate killing, except for personal reasons, is a last resort. Murder, open or suspected: sins against the religious code: persistent misbehaviour, like constantly running after other men's wives in spite of repeated warnings—any of these may be viewed as capital offences.

Rather different is private vengeance, often demanded of kinsmen or clansfolk. Then feuds may go on for one generation after another, with spasmodic killings or accusations of sorcery. But on the northern Arnhem Land coast we find the *magarada*, a special peace-making ceremony. When everyone is painted and ready, the chosen or self-confessed offender must face a barrage of spears from his victim's relatives. Occasionally he is killed: but often a wound or two is enough to satisfy his accusers.

In every case, the means of maintaining law and order is more or less localized in scope. Sanctions and decisions valid within a clan, a tribe, a linguistic group, have no binding force outside it. Only when a number of groups are linked in a common culture pattern or trading alliance, or acknowledge a common sacred and ceremonial bond, do they have any wider application. Religious cults, faith in the Beings who set the pattern of living—these carry with them their own ethical codes, their conceptions of right and wrong. But they are not universal. Even the Ancestral Beings themselves have authority only in regions where their rites are performed, where people believe in their power and their sacred origin.

But if the picture once was of scattered local groups, each autonomous and convinced of its own superiority, today that picture is changing. The old laws are passing; and the white man's authority, enforced in almost every part of the Continent, is all but supreme.

55. An artist painting his *wuramu* pole, depicting an Indonesian of historic times. It is used in *jiridja* moiety mortuary rituals. Elcho Island, 1964.

56. Non-secret *pulapa* dancing relating to the mythic being Papalu, of Wailbri origin. Conical headdresses tipped with feathers are constructed on a basis of brush and bark, bound with fibre and superimposed with feather-down designs: a 'bucket' type headdress is decorated in the same way. Near Ernabella, Musgrave Ranges, 1969.

Photograph: courtesy N. M. Wallace

Above: 57. Dancers with conical headdresses performing the *pulapa*. Nea Ernabella, Musgrave Ranges, 1969.
Photograph: courtesy N. M. Wallace

Left: 58. Dancing in a circumcision ritual (*djunggawon*) at Elcho Island, north-eastern Arnhem Land, 1966.

59. Dancing in the same circumcision ritual held on Elcho Island early in 1966. The dancers use pronged fishing spears, symbolically spearing fish, represented by a piece of bark. Behind are ceremonial flags and onlookers.

60. Terminating a ritual circumcision sequence, a group of men call invocations to the spirits. On the right stands the singing leader with his clapping sticks. Elcho Island, 1966.

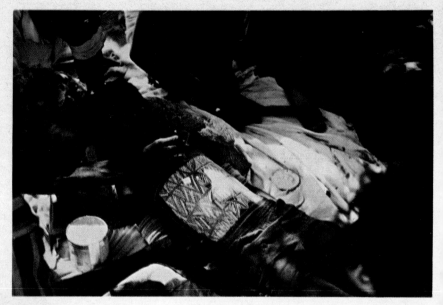

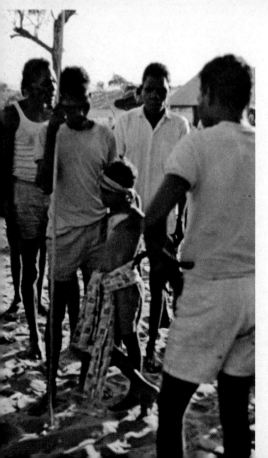

Above: 61. A circumcision novice is
painted with sacred clan designs.
Similar designs are painted on bar[
Elcho Island, 1966.

Left: 62. A circumcision novice: n
surround him to call invocations,
before the actual rite. Elcho Island
1966.

CHAPTER XVI

Behaving

NON-literate peoples, we are sometimes told, experience the sexual urge more strongly than do members of the great Western civilizations with their wide range of interests and distractions: their notions of morality are poorly defined, their concepts of right and wrong based on expediency or self-interest and distorted by sectional control. Early writers on the Australian Aborigines uncritically adopted this point of view. Even those who emphasized the strictness of formal marriage rules seemed to feel that the Aborigines were over-interested in matters of sex, with most of their ceremonies merely an excuse for sexual licence. Travellers and settlers found that native men readily offered their womenfolk, and the women themselves showed no reluctance: and so the legend of their looseness gained ground. It was not clearly recognized then, that European standards are not universally valid: a people may fail to conform to them and yet may be morally strict according to its own code of behaviour.

So it was, and is, with the Aborigines, where freedom of sexual expression is constantly restricted by religious and kinship sanctions to traditionally accepted forms of decency. One is continually aware of the frank importance the Aborigines attach to the sexual aspect: with a few reservations, they have little privacy in matters of this kind. Sexual behaviour, they feel, is not a topic which must be deliberately veiled or virtually ignored in a community. The physical relations between men and women are spoken of freely and with little or no embarrassment, even in mixed company or in the presence of children: for sex is considered a necessary and a natural factor in human life.

To people like ourselves, accustomed to wearing clothes, the naked body enhances and stresses the sexual character-istics. But among the Aborigines, who before contact went naked or wore only the minimum of covering, such a commonplace sight would not of itself arouse sexual feeling. Except in individual cases of personal attraction, the criterion here was a sexually provocative posture.

Erotic stimulation, however, is practised at times. In many areas there are (or were) secular ceremonies, where men and women in turn choose sweethearts from among the dancers, and couples slip away together into the shadows. There are erotic jokes and allusions, and frank love songs which leave little to the imagination. And the great fertility rituals often involve sexual licence on the sacred ground, when ordinary kinship tabus and pro-hibitions are ignored or deliberately flouted. A man may be intimate then with his tribal mother-in-law, whom in normal times he must strictly avoid, or with his tribal sister: and so strong is the force of convention and public opinion that it is rarely anyone declines to take part.

A woman who has looked at or fingered one of the men's secret emblems should, as a rule, forfeit her life, and her kin may not avenge her death. But in some places she is offered first an alternative choice. If she is willing to go out into the Bush, making herself available to all the local men for as long as they wish, the episode will be overlooked and no more will be said. Some women accept the offer casually as nothing out of the way: but others, especially if they have absorbed the European attitude (in theory at least) that extra-marital relations must at all costs be avoided, have been speared for resisting.

Where convention sanctions affairs of this kind, husband or wife should raise no objection. Jealousy, as a rule, is confined to individual liaisons. So, on ceremonial occasions or when a tribal brother is visiting, a man may lend or exchange his wife as a matter of course: and everyone, in fact, seems to appreciate the break in monotony. It was this feature which led the early settlers, when women were offered to them as a friendly gesture with an eye to future benefits, to speak scornfully of the Aborigines' immorality and greed.

Nevertheless, within their own particular code, these First Australians prize circumspect behaviour. Young boys at initiation are warned against indiscriminate entanglements: and girls are advised that a woman should be modest, shy of strangers and of men other than her own husband and his tribal brothers. Walking or resting she must see that her loin covering is neatly adjusted; dancing in the main camp, in mixed company, she must nearly always keep her head lowered and her eyes demurely downcast. There are exceptions, of course. Whatever the ideal, women are often noisy and self-assertive: and a few here and there have a reputation for boldness.

When scattered family groups gather together for ceremonies or for trade there may be a young woman or

107

two bent on flirtation. Her husband is old, perhaps, and lets her amuse herself provided she is discreet. She will dawdle as she passes in front of a young man: swaying her hips, smiling and staring at him before she coyly lowers her lashes. This is an easy way to obtain lovers; although even if her husband is complaisant his relatives, or her own father, may decide that she needs discipline. She may be scolded or beaten, or taken into the Bush with a group of men to 'quieten' her. (If she wants sexual experience, they say in effect, she shall have it.) In stubborn cases she may be wounded or killed—the usual punishment, too, for a man who constantly seeks sweethearts. Other women, more cautious or more restrained, may resent her: and their comments are sharper when they fear their own husbands may respond to her charms.

'Look at her!' scoffed a couple of women in northern Arnhem Land, watching a young girl hurrying lightly down the beach. 'This is how she walks!' (They moved their shoulders, throwing their breasts forward and exaggeratedly swinging their hips.) 'Every time she sees some man looking at her, she runs into the water and splashes about. We know why she does it. Hasn't she got a husband?' 'She walks like a pussycat,' sneered another, brought up on a Mission station. 'She's always looking for men!'

Here as among ourselves, the public opinion, which reinforces the rules of propriety, is based on a number of motives which often go unsuspected. Jealousy, possessiveness, envy or spite may find expression in this anxiety to see that others conform. And shame is a potent force in ensuring obedience to the demands of convention.

Pre-marital and extra-marital freedom is tolerated within specified limits: beyond these, it is discouraged. Men and women may 'swear' in anger or grief, using obscene terms, or words usually uttered only during certain sacred rituals: but for the most part only extreme provocation is accepted as an excuse. Children in many tribes may speak and behave with the utmost freedom, abusing and even striking their elders with no consistent punishment: but once they reach puberty, or go through their initiation, they are expected to know better.

A moral adult is, broadly speaking, one who participates fully in the sacred rituals: is industrious in hunting and food collecting, hospitable and generous within a recognized circle, and quick to fulfil economic and social obligations. He (or she) is faithful to his marriage partner, or partners, in the local sense of the term: for marriage here does not involve forsaking all others, and he may have occasional sweethearts provided he keeps to the rules. He does not fight continually with his wife, nor beat her without clear provocation. He is not quarrelsome or a bully, but he can employ force to defend his interests or support those of his kin. In some tribes he can go further than this, bluffing or using his spears to obtain what he wants, or manipulating his obligations to suit himself. He does not, as a rule, fall back on sorcery: but even this is approved by some groups as a legitimate weapon.

Today, with new ideas and values gaining acceptance, the old code of ethics cannot remain unchanged. But the picture here is often disturbed. Missionaries, settlers, police, and casual visitors may present different and even conflicting points of view, so that the Aborigines finally adopt some kind of compromise. Promiscuity, in places, has followed the breakdown of traditional sanctions: for the old controls were based on group action and ultimately on supernatural punishment or reward, and relied hardly at all on the individual conscience. The transition from one pattern of behaviour, clear cut and compact for all its rigidity,[11] to the fluctuating and internally inconsistent

109

code which we have to offer, has not always been happy. They may conform, superficially; but unless they accept in some measure the values on which their new behaviour is based, the collapse of their old system will find them unprepared and confused.

The Thunder Man; from a bark drawing, western Arnhem Land.

CHAPTER XVII

Magic and Sorcery

THE very word 'magic' conjures up exciting possibilities; even the sceptic is conscious of its glamour. But to the people who practise it, people who feel that they can project their own desires on to others and make them come true, it has the reality of everyday experience.

'White' or harmless magic, 'black' magic or sorcery—nearly every Aboriginal tribe has practised either or both. Sometimes they must be performed by special people—the native doctor, or a grown man or woman well-versed in magical knowledge. But in many regions anyone past adolescence who knows what to do may attempt them, secretly or in public.

Notorious out of all proportion to the area it covers is the so-called 'pointing-bone' of the inland, used ritually to inflict sickness or death from a distance. But the object itself is only a symbol. Far more significant is the curse, the spell, with an independent power of its own which can be released by uttering or chanting it in the proper way.

Often the spell, by itself, is strong enough to have the desired result. But to make doubly sure, the sorcerer often makes use of an object of some kind as well: the 'bone'; a rough model of the victim in beeswax or bound paperbark; nail parings, a lock of his hair, anything that has been in close personal contact with him. As this melts or burns in the fire, rots in the ground, or gradually breaks up as it swings from a tree, so the victim weakens and finally dies. Alternatively, the sorcerer may draw the victim in coloured ochres on the wall of a cave, repeating his name, and singing some creature to destroy him. Or he may subject him to a ritual operation, removing his kidney fat, or plunging a sharp fine stick downwards from his collar bone to pierce his heart. Once the victim's spirit has left him, the death of his body is never delayed for long.

The only hope of cure is to find some native doctor powerful enough to combat the malignant influence of the sorcerer. But this can be done only if matters have not been left for too long. A native doctor will not risk his reputation by trying to cure a dying man or woman, unless he is confident of success.

When a man or woman is killed in an open fight, or dies after a spear wound, everyone can be reasonably certain what caused his death. But in cases of illness and accident, snake bite and drowning, they are not so sure. The immediate cause is clear enough: they can see the physical signs and perhaps they were present when the crocodile the shark or the snake attacked.

But this is not enough. What brought about the disease? What led the creature to choose that particular victim? Physical symptoms, so the Aborigines believe, are only secondary: for the body is dependent on the spirit, and much less important. Malicious thoughts and intentions act first upon the spirit—the physical damage comes later.

Left : 63. The Elcho Island Memorial in 1958. This was the focus of an Adjustment Movement, now channelized into a Council. These carved and painted poles are sacred clan emblems, the designs being rich in mythical symbolism.

Below : 64. Making a Morning Star emblem for a Morning Star ceremony. Elcho Island, 1968. This symbolizes the star(s) sent by spirits of the dead from the mythical *dua* moiety island of Bralgu.

65. Women dancing in a mortuary ritual. They hold seagull-feathered string attached to the sacred emblems—the arms of the spirit beings that these represent. Yirrkalla, north-eastern Arnhem Land, 1968.

66. Part of the mortuary sequence shown above, for a Riradjingu headman who died late in 1967. In the beach camp at Yirrkalla, 1968, sacred *dua* moiety emblems associated with the Wawalag (Wauwalak) mythology have been revealed, prior to dancing. Note feathered tassels hanging from the poles. The bucket at one end of the didjeridu makes the sound more resonant.

67. Didjeridu player, and songman beating his clapping sticks. Goulburn Island, western Arnhem Land, 1961.

68. Part of a *jiridja* moiety mortuary ritual: the central dancer postures with a *wuramu* figure representing the dead man. Yirrkalla, north-eastern Arnhem Land, 1968.

69. Group of singers in *jiridja* moiety mortuary ritual, beside a
bugulub ground plan depicting the sacred totemic and mythic site of
the deceased. Yirrkalla, 1964.

70. Men performing the 'handkerchief dance', in a *jiridja* moiety
mortuary sequence. The flags are symbols of farewell to the deceased's
spirit, and one bears an anchor design; these relate to the 'Macassan'
song cycle. Yirrkalla, 1964.

The treatment, therefore, must be directed along these lines. The native doctor diagnoses the trouble from a non-material point of view. His efforts are aimed at healing or recapturing the victim's spirit; and once that is done, the body should revive and grow healthy again. He may use massage or sucking, pretending to extract the malignant substance in concrete form, as a stone or a stick: and remedies for many minor complaints, natural medicines like special roots and plants, may be found in the Bush. But the emphasis in healing is on the spirit: and the victim must have faith in the native doctor, as an essential part of the 'cure'. The psychological effect of the healing rites is often of major importance.

Not all native doctors, or 'clever men', are equally powerful, whether or not they know all the tricks of their trade. They are endowed with power only after years of preparation and training, with a special form of initiation involving ritual death and rebirth. They must undergo various ritual operations, with magical pearl-shells or spirit-sticks inserted into their bodies.

A really competent native doctor with a wide reputation is an impressive figure. He is poised and self-confident, aware of his vital responsibility: and often, but not always, he is a ceremonial leader as well. Even outside his own tribe, perhaps, he is much in demand—not only for healing, but also for making rain, foretelling the future, divining at a death, or counteracting the evil effects of sorcery.

As a rule, he will not practise 'black' magic himself, although some native doctors have done so from time to time—especially in the contact situation.

Nor does he use love magic, found in various forms all over Australia. Perhaps a man or woman is unhappy in marriage, anxious to recapture the affection of wife or husband: or trying to keep a lover, or wanting a new one.

113

To meet this need there are love charms and spells, and whole series of semi-magical songs. One person may work alone, more or less secretly. Or a group of men or a group of women may gather to help one another, singing and perhaps dancing together to achieve what they want. Some of the songs are linked with big religious cults that stress human and animal fertility—just as the well-known *tjarada* love singing merges into the sacred Kunapipi.

Ordinary people can practise rain magic too, especially important in the dry inland 'deserts'; they may scrape a pearl-shell, perhaps, or chant special spells. They can sing to halt or prevent quarrels, to heal sickness and wounds, to ensure success in hunting and fishing, to avert snakes, and (often in semi-religious context) to bring about seasonal increase.

Their personal desires can find expression in magic, enhancing their self-confidence and their assurance of satisfaction. If nothing happens, showing their 'power' is too weak or their knowledge deficient, then they can call on the native doctor. And if all else fails, they can fall back on sorcery—the final resort of a frustrated or angry person who cannot achieve what he wants by any other legitimate means.

Nobody will admit, openly, practising sorcery—for he, or she, would meet with vengeance sooner or later. But it remains a possibility, a weapon which 'others' have used to fulfil their own desires. And in times of stress, when the life that people have known seems to be slipping from their grasp, the growing emphasis on sorcery is a sign of their confusion. No longer a sanction against anti-social behaviour, it becomes not only a means of attacking the white man, but a source of dissension and conflict among themselves—not only a symptom, but also a secondary cause of tribal disunity.

CHAPTER XVIII

Death and What Follows

DEATH is the final crisis, from which there is no ritual re-birth. But through it a man or woman becomes really sacred, in a way not possible to the living even in the most sacred of ceremonies.

Close relatives grieve at a baby's death: but the loss of an adult or older child is mourned by the whole community. Kinsfolk and campfellows wail and sob, gashing themselves with spears and knives, axes or sharp stones, until the blood flows. The loudest crying, the most violent self-mutilation, come from the dead man's immediate family—for here their sorrow and anguish, their helpless anger, can find release in socially accepted ways. Others not so deeply affected join them in the conventional expression of grief, actively showing their sympathy and regret, and at the same time paying attention to the deceased's spirit.

Soon the whole camp moves away from the scene of the death: the dead man's name becomes tabu, at least for a year or so, and all his possessions may be ritually destroyed. If he has not been killed openly, there is a search for the supposed murderer: and various tabus are imposed on the closest mourners.

But first the body must be disposed of—buried or cremated, mummified or dessicated: exposed on a special platform of branches, or stood upright with outstretched arms tied to a tree. As a rule, it is specially treated beforehand—smeared with red ochre, perhaps, or painted on chest and face with totemic designs: and most of the hair may be cut, to make into waist bands.

Some tribes practised burial cannibalism—in parts of Queensland and the northern Kimberleys, on the southwest of the Gulf of Carpentaria, and in north-east South Australia. Among the Liverpool River people in western Arnhem Land, certain relatives eat a little of the dead person's flesh in the hope of absorbing something of his spirit. And in Central Australia a mother may consume the flesh of a still-born child, so that its spirit may be born again through her.

Many rituals and ceremonies follow a death, sometimes continuing spasmodically for months or years. Each tribe, or group of tribes, has its own views of what should be done, its conception of the needs of spirit and mourners.

The mourners may share in a huge mortuary feast, with singing and dancing to help the spirit on its way to the land of the dead. When the bones are dry they may be collected and cleaned, as in northern Arnhem Land, and placed in a small bark coffin painted with totemic patterns. Later they may be inserted ritually, one by one, into a huge carved and painted log coffin, twenty feet long or more, which is lifted upright in the camp and left to rot. The eastern Arnhem Landers, too, carve special wooden grave posts—usually stylized images of the deceased, smaller and less spectacular than those of Bathurst and Melville Islands. Or a mast is raised over the grave as a symbol of farewell, just as the Indonesian traders on the north coast once erected their masts and unfurled their sails before returning home.

To all the Aborigines, death marks the end only of bodily existence: for the spirit, or soul, is indestructible. Sometimes it was thought to have many forms, but more often two—the soul itself, often with partly totemic significance; and a trickster spirit, often malignant to humankind.

In the Great Victoria Desert, the spirit which first animated the dead man's embryo finally escapes from his body at death. For some time it wanders near the camp, and after burial lingers about the grave. At last the re-burial party drives it into the grave, where the widow or widower, or some close relative, speaks to it in conventional terms. Later on it may serve as spiritual informant to a native doctor, in foretelling future events and in divination, before returning to the spirit centre, from which it may enter some woman to be re-born. But its counterpart, the trickster spirit, wanders indefinitely, causing much annoyance to tribesfolk.

In other parts of Australia, in the east, west and north-west, the spirit was said to go eventually into the sky, where it remained with the Creative Beings. Others believed that it returned to its original spirit-centre, becoming identified with its totem, or lived near the sacred site associated with some particular Being. On the Lower River Murray, spirits of the dead travelled by a defined track along the coast and across the sea to a mythical island. The soul of a dead western Arnhem Lander may be met by a Spirit Being who tries to kill (or completely annihilate) it; but usually it escapes. Then, in return for a fee of one kind or another, it may be ferried by canoe across the water to the land of the dead, where it undergoes further tests and finally joins the Ancestors. For the northern Arnhem Landers, there are two islands of the dead, one in the Torres Straits or somewhere north of the Wessels, the other beyond the sunrise at the island of Bralgu, the last halting place of the Djanggawul Beings on their journey to the Australian coast. Even so, part of the soul returns to the clan well; and part roams the land as a trickster spirit.

But whether the spirit remains near its former kinsfolk and countrymen, or travels to some special land of the dead, it never loses its link with the living. All members of a tribe, a clan, a totemic 'country', are united spiritually by ties which cannot be severed at death: for all are part of one whole, sharing a common past and a common future within the ever-present Eternal Dreamtime.

Two nude women dancing: from a brown-paper drawing, west-central Northern Territory.

CHAPTER XIX

Values

BEHIND all this elaborate framework, this variegated pattern of external behaviour, lie the beliefs, the values, which give it animation and purpose.

The tribe, or the clan, is not an impersonal unit, acting mechanically. The individuals who comprise it are not automatons, going through their rituals and songs, their kinship obligations and marriage rules, under a sort of blind compulsion. Everything they do, or say, springs from an emotional background which colours their whole conception of life, and motivates all their actions. Even the fundamental drives of food and sex are modified and shaped within this context, so that their expression is never quite the same from one society to another.

A child growing up into the life of his people absorbs their values, their attitudes, as he does the outward signs of conformity. For in an Aboriginal group there is no basic conflict of opinions: religious and traditional sanctions, governing even everyday behaviour, ensure an

119

overall unity of action and thought. These values are not always made clear in words. They may have been part of life for so long, accepted by each generation in turn, that they are finally taken for granted: never discussed, never questioned, but assumed to be inevitable and immutable.

The Aborigines' attitude towards material goods, for instance, has irritated many hundreds of settlers who do not share it. Their lack of emphasis on accumulating possessions, on making settled homes, is notorious. Superficially, it has overshadowed the tremendous complexity of their social and sacred life.

But their absence of wealth as we define it, their semi-nomadic wanderings, are only part of the total situation. They are symptoms, in fact, of the Aborigines' close relationship with their environment, on which they depend for their very existence—for we must remember that they have never been planters or cultivators, nor herders of cattle or sheep, but people who relied entirely on the foods which they gathered from land and sea.

This physical need bred an emotional dependence as well, a spiritual bond with their own country and its natural resources. In many parts of Australia it has led to a special emphasis in religious life—a concept of various Creative Beings whose power can ensure the fertility of the earth which supplies them with food: of the rhythmic coming and going of the seasons, the death and re-birth of animals and plants, the continuity of life in all its forms.

And part of this concept is expressed in the Aborigines' view of life as a continuum, a whole, not sharply divided into definite points of time—a view often summarized in the phrase 'Eternal Dreaming', or 'Eternal Dreamtime'. Although for everyday purposes they distinguish between past, present and future, in sacred and ritual life they regard these three phases as being essentially one. The

Above: 71. Women stand up to dance in the *jiridja* moiety mortuary ritual. Their hand and body and dancing-string movements traditionally match the appropriate songs. Yirrkalla, 1964.

Left: 72. Posturing before the flags erected in a *jiridja* moiety mortuary ritual. One flag bears traditional emblemic designs. Yirrkalla, 1964.

Right: 73. Dancing before the
farewelling flags, *jiridja*
moiety mortuary ritual.
Yirrkalla, 1964.

Below: 74. Collective dancing
in *jiridja* moiety mortuary
ritual. Yirrkalla, 1964.

75. An incident in the *kulama* yam series. A group of participants rub crushed *kulama* and ochre over their bodies. At one side is a painted bark basket. Melville Island, 1954.
Courtesy C. P. Mountford

76. Man observing a *pukamani* tabu, associated with mourning; he may not touch food, but is being fed. Snake Bay, Melville Island, 1969.
Photograph: courtesy M. Brandl

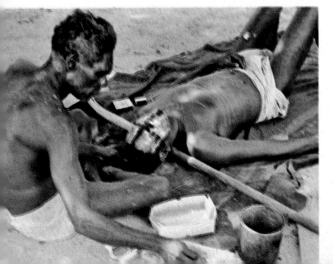

77. Painting a typical *pukamani* mortuary mask on one of the performers. Snake Bay, Melville Island, 1969.
Photograph: courtesy M. Brandl

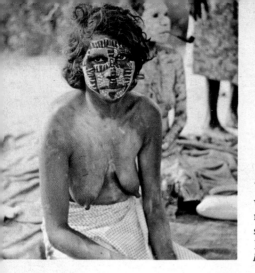

78. Woman decorated by her father with a painted mask for the *pukamani* rituals. The design represents a natural species of mythic origin. Snake Bay, Melville Island, 1969.
Photograph: courtesy M. Brandl

79. Woman decorated for the *pukamani* rituals, wearing a *tokwianga* ball around her neck. Snake Bay, Melville Island, 1969.
Photograph: courtesy M. Brandl

80. Chief mourners in a *pukamani* mortuary sequence. The central kneeling participant wears a false beard. The suitcase contains the dead person's clothing. Bathurst Island, 1969.
Photograph: courtesy M. Brandl

Creative Beings are, in this sense, 'eternal'. They are as much alive today, spiritually, as they were in the beginning of time when they walked the earth; and they will continue to live in the future, as long as human life endures. In this ever-present 'stream' of time belong the Aborigines themselves, for their spirits too are eternal.

Upon this view of the universe, based on their own physical and spiritual needs, the Aborigines built their world.

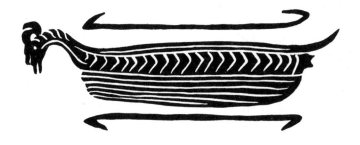

The Rainbow Snake; from a bark drawing, Oenpelli, western Arnhem Land.

Waves coming up: high waves coming up
 against the rocks,
Breaking, shi! shi!
When the moon is high with its light upon the
 waters:
Spring tide; tide flowing to the grass,
Breaking, shi! shi!
In its rough waters, the young girls bathe.
Hear the sound they make with their hands
 as they play!

(A Laragia traditional song: now a lament for the country which is
no longer theirs.)

CHAPTER XX

The Changing World

EVEN before the white man came to Australia, some of the Aborigines had come into contact with aliens.

People at the north of Cape York Peninsula met Torres Strait Islanders and Melanesians. And on the north Australian coast, especially in eastern Arnhem Land, Indonesian traders were constant visitors over hundreds of years, until the Commonwealth Government intervened at the beginning of this century.

From their long association, the Indonesians regarded Arnhem Land and its islands as rightfully theirs, and the white settlers as interlopers. And they were, in fact, the first discoverers and exploiters of this country apart from the Aborigines themselves. They came down in their thousands, fleets of praus blowing down on the north-west monsoon which heralded the wet season: and on the mainland they established settlements, building stilted huts where they lived for about five to six months, until the 'dry' wind from the south-east came to help them on their homeward journey. During their stay they employed and traded with local Aborigines, gathering supplies of trepang and pearl-shell, sandalwood and turtle shell. Some of the Arnhem Landers went on the praus to Macassar and the Indonesian islands, and saw something of the outside world: and a few even settled down there, and never returned to Australia.

Not all the coastal tribes today show the same effects of this contact. Some seem to have been scarcely influenced at all: while others, like the northern and north-eastern Arnhem Landers, adopted various new traits into their own way of life—carved wooden figures, exotic songs, and a special series of myths.

The north coast had Japanese traders as well, and inland there were large camps of Chinese coolies and labourers: but none of these, with their relatively restricted numbers and less intensive contact, had the same disruptive consequences as the settlement of Australia by Europeans.

From the fertile south, white settlers and explorers spread across the Continent: and the result, for the Aborigines, was gradual detribalization, depopulation, and disillusionment. They were herded into artificial surroundings—settlements and camps where they were forced to create a new life for themselves, with little constructive help.

In consequence, we find today scattered pockets of full-bloods who have almost lost their traditional background; only partially adjusted to our way of living, they have no hope of returning to the old Aboriginal way. Others again are living in very much the same way as their forefathers did—but they are in the minority. At the other end of the scale there are isolated families or small groups in country towns, with only their dark skin, their memories, and perhaps a few words of their own tongue, to mark their link with the past. And then there are the mixed-bloods, the part-Aborigines—from the child in an outback native camp, through the bewildered man and woman caught between the demands of two worlds, to those completely assimilated, looking at life through the eyes of the white man.

Some points in the process seem to be broadly the same.

At first the Aborigines, dazzled perhaps by the white man's apparent wealth, want to see and know more about him—and take what he has to offer. But they are not always discriminating in their choice of friends or of goods; and hindered by language barriers, and by the limitations of their own background, they may find the results disappointing. They are not fully accepted in the new situation, and they do not understand much of the new life that comes their way. Knowing that they do not belong, but feeling powerless to do anything about it, they become at last frustrated and disillusioned.

They may try, then, to find help, encouragement and faith among their own people, discovering too late that in their eagerness to grasp at the white man's cultural heritage they have lost their own.

A tribe or a small local group may be in more or less constant association with some white man or other. Gradually control shifts into his hands, until he becomes the dominant local authority. He may be a missionary, a settler, or a Government official; but in practice, though not always in theory, he comes to take charge of their lives. In cases of murder, or offences against the white men themselves, the police intervene; but even apart from this, both sacred and non-sacred laws of the tribe are affected by the change.

Now the old people, once valued for their experience and wisdom, can offer little positive help; and the force of traditional mythology loses its potency in the face of introduced standards and values. Eventually, it no longer

125

suffices to maintain group cohesion and solidarity: and when nothing comparable has been introduced to take its place, the society must collapse. As long as the introduced code remains external, not emotionally significant to the Aborigines, it cannot function effectively.

As authority passes from the family, the clan or tribe, to the stranger, there is a growing emphasis on individual instead of on group responsibility. This involves a drastic change in the system of maintaining law and order, leading to increased interference from outside: and that, in turn, has further repercussions on the Aborigines' ability to control their own internal affairs.

There are, of course, some exceptions. Not all the Aborigines become disillusioned, despite the changes they see taking place around them. Much depends on the way in which their life was oriented before, and on the extent of their contact with aliens over the years. The northern Arnhem Landers, accustomed to constant Indonesian visitors, their horizons widened to include not only Indonesia but the Torres Straits, and even southern New Guinea, have so far managed to retain their cultural identity in spite of fairly intensive white contact. But the inland 'desert' people, with their limited view of the outside world, have not been able to withstand the shock of the impact.

Each type of contact has its own peculiar effects on the people subjected to it. A man or woman influenced over a long period by Mission contact will have rather a different outlook from one brought up in a city or town. So will a person who has grown up in the atmosphere of some old style cattle station—an atmosphere, insofar as he is concerned, of petty quarrels, of bullying, hatred, seduction, and killing: who has worked without wages, inadequately fed and clothed, watching his tribesfolk losing interest in their own traditions and rituals.

126

But for these Aborigines, these First Australians, contact need not mean death. They are not doomed by some mysterious law to vanish, inevitably, from the white man's world.

Certainly, over the greater part of the Continent, this has been the case in the past. But the causes have been, in most cases, ignorance and thoughtlessness rather than deliberate cruelty. We should know better now, learning from the mistakes of the past century, from the experience of other countries which have indigenous peoples. And for the Aborigines who are left, it need not be too late.

They cannot continue to live in their old way, and indeed few of them are able to do so now. Life is changing for them just as it is, in a different sense, for us: and the white man is the new power in the land. It seems certain that they must, in the coming generations, become more fully absorbed into the main stream of Australian life.

But they have something to offer us, too—something of their vitality and colour, the spiritual heritage of the Aboriginal Way. Enriched by this link with their traditional background, we can become more truly Australian, more deeply a part of this land which we, like the Aborigines, know and love.

127

CHAPTER XXI

The Future

IN THE Preface to this new edition we drew attention to some of the changes that have been taking place in the last few years—changes that have been far-reaching, and are likely to be even more so.

Aboriginal welfare and administration are officially still the concern of the various States, with the Commonwealth directly responsible only for the Northern Territory—a formal arrangement still required by the Constitution. Nevertheless, for practical purposes this impediment has to some extent been by-passed. Closer co-operation between the respective departments involved has gone hand in hand with greater uniformity in policy and in practice, so that for the first time we can really begin to speak of 'Australian' policy here. The key word is 'begin', because difficulties still remain. But on this issue, at least, Commonwealth and States have been coming together, and not merely in discussions around a conference table.

Pressures from outside as well as from within Australia

81. *Pukamani* mortuary dancing. Bathurst Island, 1969
Photograph: courtesy M. Brandl

82. Principal *pukamani* dancer, decorated with mask-like facial design and feathered headdress. He wears a false *baludi* beard and holds a *tokwianga* ball in his mouth. Bathurst Island, 1969.
Photograph: courtesy M. Brandl

83. Principal male dancer and mourners before the deceased's possessions in the *pukamani* rituals. Bathurst Island, 1969.
Photograph: courtesy M. Brandl

84. A group of newly erected mortuary posts. Snake Bay, 1968.
Photograph: courtesy M. Brandl

85. A group of weather-worn mortuary posts, after completion of relevant rituals. Snake Bay, 1968.
Photograph: courtesy M. Brandl

have helped to speed these developments. In the sphere of regulations and laws, special restrictions affecting Aborigines are almost a thing of the past. Originally planned to protect and safeguard a people in special need of protection, they were becoming ends in themselves, consolidating and ramifying. The official emphasis on welfare was being lost in a maze of prohibitions. The straightening out of this tangled pattern—an uneven blend of suppression and encouragement—was long overdue.

People of Aboriginal descent now receive Social Service benefits on the same basis as other Australians. They are eligible to enrol as voters—a point especially significant in certain northern electorates where they make up a clear majority. It is not only as a subject of welfare policies that they are becoming politically important. More specifically, they can anticipate a stronger share of bargaining power in the competitive domain of State and Commonwealth politics. Candidates will be more eager, now, to secure their goodwill, which in the past was viewed mainly with indifference or even hostility.

For all but a few regions, the long-standing argument over the 'right to drink' has been settled—at least to the point where the problems it poses are not peculiar to Aborigines. The controversial issue of citizenship is almost resolved. Facilities for primary and secondary education and for technical training are vastly improved; and this means that far more Aboriginal students can be expected to enter the universities—whereas now the funds available to them, official and otherwise, greatly exceed the demand. Compensation for the development of mineral and other resources has become more than a distant ideal, and in some areas royalties have already been paid. Even the long-dormant issue of Aboriginal land rights has been revived, stimulated by the finding of

129

bauxite deposits on two northern reserves. And although Aborigines are still officially excluded from the Commonwealth Census reports, this exclusion is due to an outdated section of the Constitution on which an early referendum is hoped for (no Constitutional amendment can be made without referendum). It is reasonable to expect that this referendum will result in official inclusion of Aboriginal population details in the Census results. In the past, various attempts have been made by official census-takers to count persons of Aboriginal descent; but it is only in the last few years that these attempts have been at all comprehensive. Like figures and estimates compiled by local centres such as mission and government settlements and pastoral stations, and by the State and Commonwealth departments responsible for Aboriginal welfare, these assessments of the Aboriginal population have been valid only up to a point. In the 1966 Census, counting of Aborigines took place on a much more systematic and extensive basis than before, and the results of that effort are to appear in a separate publication.

But legislation and formal provisions of this kind are not enough, even when backed up by a better command of skills and techniques and brighter prospects of employment. They set a framework for action, and limits to exploitation—ideally, at least. Beyond that, responsibility rests with the people involved: on the one hand, the dominant population; on the other, those who identify themselves or are identified by others as being, wholly or in part, of Aboriginal descent. What is vaguely called 'public opinion' can bring pressure to bear on politicians and legislators; but it can also nullify the most humane of laws. In Australia today, as far as one can tell, the force of popular opinion sustains the official ruling that there should be no legal discrimination on the grounds of race

—that, for instance, nobody should be excluded on that score from any school or other institution, or restaurant, or hotel, or any public vehicle or place. This is the premise underlying the policy of 'assimilation', accepted in principle by both Commonwealth and States.

Official policy aside, popular attitudes may yet have to undergo a major test.

One such test, it seems from the experience in other countries, is a massive alteration in scale, or population ratio, not necessarily spread over a whole region. Australia is still far from a crisis in this sense, and if official hopes are realized, its population will become in time so completely unified, if not unitary, that this contingency could not arise. Mild alarm was voiced when, just before the second world war, the number of part-Aborigines was seen to be rising—not as a result of mixed unions, but because they were finding mates among themselves. It was this, their failure to merge into the total population, that caused concern, and not their numerical growth in itself.

The population explosion among 'full bloods' is much more recent, and much less localized than it seemed at first. Accompanied as it is by a rate of increase higher than that of Australians in general, it certainly has implications for the future. Official efforts to build 'a single Australian community' (to quote from a statement on assimilation policy) were inspired, not by an abstract ideal, but by a sense of practical urgency. The aim is that, regardless of racial or cultural background, all Australians should be equal at law, as citizens: that in this sense the question of race should be irrelevant.

It is comfortably easy to be tolerant when there are no serious clashes of interest, when the minority population is a minority in numbers as well as in power, and when differences appear small or ephemeral. Thus, in the early

131

days of settlement, the British Colonial Office could remain physically and emotionally aloof from the depressing reality of relations between Europeans and Aborigines in Australia: it could afford to express liberal sentiments which most of the settlers on the spot did not share. Now, so many years later, much the same sentiments have a very wide currency indeed.

There are still pockets of dissent. All of these have been under fire for some time but, until recently, with little effect. They are essentially survivals of the pioneering days when Aborigines and Europeans came to terms simply on the basis of expediency—when each made use of the other's services, or goods, or persons, but tried to keep the main part of its 'private' life distinct and separate. In pastoral areas of the north, for example, a quasi-feudal system has been fighting a losing battle for survival; in the current basic-wage issue, the practical working out of the proposed changes there is both more and less than a simple question of economics.

The people who gathered around the pastoral stations found themselves becoming anchored there. Their freedom of movement was restricted. Habit, desire for new goods and new foods, and the strength of family ties, helped to hold them. But there were other pressures too, and one of these was the claim that they 'belonged' to one station rather than to another. A good employee was an economic asset, jealously guarded. A 'gentlemen's agreement' among neighbouring stations, backed by threat of force, safeguarded the rights of his employer; and although a few strayed, many did not. For the most part, in lieu of regular wages he and his dependants received their keep, and a few extras. The picture in this respect has varied—for instance, between some of the smaller owner-occupied stations, and the larger holdings where absentee landlords lacked personal contact with

European as well as Aboriginal employees. Since the second world war, however, things have not been the same in the north. Payment of at least a nominal wage, more in some cases, kept trouble at bay for a time—especially since the powerful trade unions based in the southern cities seemed reluctant to become deeply involved. But the argument of 'equal pay for equal work' is now being openly raised. The counter-arguments which challenged it for so long—that Aboriginal labour was largely unskilled, and that care of dependants (wives, children, old people, the physically incapacitated) made it essentially unprofitable—have been eroded, in the first place by the spread of schools and specialized training programmes, and in the second by government provision of Social Service benefits.

The Commonwealth Arbitration Commission has ruled that the full pastoral award wage is to apply in the Northern Territory from December 1968; but strikes on two stations there have helped to force an agreement that, as an interim measure, skilled stockmen should receive full award rates from November 1966. Western Australia can be expected eventually to follow the Commonwealth lead, with all that this portends for the pastoral situation in the Kimberleys. Throughout this field, the slow rate of change in the past is no guide to the rate of change in the future, because circumstances are now very different indeed. And among the implications, not the least is the question of the Aborigines' right of domicile on stations which many of them have come to regard as 'home'.

In the Northern Territory and in Western Australia, the fact that the main centres of government lie in the south has possibly been crucial as far as the Aborigines are concerned. As communications improved, a growing proportion of 'southerners' invaded the north—transients like administrative officials and school teachers, with no long-term stake in the politics of the local situation. Relations between Aborigines and settlers assumed different proportions when seen through the eyes of the urban south, where only the shadow of earlier clashes survived. Firm administrative control from Canberra pressed forward the Commonwealth's programme of Aboriginal welfare in the face of some local resistance; and where the Commonwealth has led, with its hand on the nation's purse strings, the States have not in this instance declined to follow.

In some 'outback' towns of the south a limited form of segregation has persisted, but the situation lacks the sharp contrasts of the north. Overall, the patterns of living show a broad similarity. There are differences, to be sure, but they are differences within a certain range. Views on hygiene, housing, employment, obligations toward relatives outside the immediate family, may not be identical for all the European-Australian and all the Aboriginal, or part-Aboriginal, inhabitants of a town, but this is a matter of degree. These are *sub*-cultural differences, and they must be seen against a framework of behaviour and assumptions which are more alike than not. There is common ground here, on which to build a wider sense of shared identity. But the impediments are far from being negligible. In part, they are a direct result of the antagonisms and restrictions of the past. Few Aborigines could escape these pressures; and those who did so were mainly the lighter-skinned part-Aborigines who could merge less conspicuously into the general population. Others, more 'visible', were correspondingly more vulnerable. Rebuffed or rejected by Europeans, they countered by withdrawal. The communities they formed in the south were not an inevitable outcome of their traditional groupings, but a response to barriers

134

THE FUTURE

imposed upon them from without, blocking them from full participation in the wider society.

Their living conditions, in these country towns and in the large cities, were more often than not well below normal Australian standards. The Europeans with whom they mixed most freely were those who were socially and economically underprivileged themselves, although not in quite the same ways and certainly not to the same degree. And although this state of affairs is changing—partly because in the more affluent society of today examples of economic hardship are less obtrusive—for many of them the broad picture still holds good.

But the 'culture of poverty', as it has been called, has a variety of facets. Its causes, and its consequences, are not everywhere identical. To say that Aboriginal and part-Aboriginal town and city dwellers behave as they do 'because' of this is misleading. Economic deprivation and a restricted range of opportunities can breed an appearance of similarity. To take this at its face value, however, is to gloss over the reasons for this situation and obscure the most appropriate means of resolving it—to submerge the specific in the general without doing justice to either.

The present is not independent of the past. Some understanding of what went on before, the combination of events and people's responses to those events, can throw light on what is happening here and now. And for people of Aboriginal descent, there are two kinds of past to be taken into account.

One belongs specifically to themselves, in so far as they *are* Aborigines: the traditional background, which for some is still real and immediate, while for others it lies well outside the range of personal experience. The second is the past of earlier contact with outsiders, one which has led directly into the present with no break in

135

continuity. Stories and reminiscences on this topic are handed on from one generation to another. In households where the old Aboriginal traditions are not even a memory, these other traditions may still persist. However much they are embellished or modified in the course of telling, they provide an emotional charter for evaluating what goes on in the contemporary scene, and especially in relation to non-Aborigines. Disappointments and slights can be interpreted in the light of this wider pattern, and in the process help to reinforce it. In this sense, the past lives on in the present. And people who are reluctant to be caught in a more competitive and more demanding world can evoke it to justify their stand.

This lack of enthusiasm for goals that many other Australians regard as important—such things as economic and occupational success and material comfort—has mostly taken the form of passive resistance, not of active opposition. For the most part, too, it has not been unrealistic: it has rested on a sober appraisal of personal chances. The prospects of success are much slighter for people who do not have the right skills, and have not had the encouragement and support of their own social circle which would drive them, first, to acquire such skills and, secondly, to use them to advantage.

If rejection of 'middle class' Australian goals depended on nothing more than absence of opportunity to reach them, the issues would be simple. It is in this field, the teaching of skills and the widening of opportunities, that current training programmes are likely to have the maximum effect. Where 'access to means' is all-important, State and Commonwealth governments have a ready answer. But there are others for whom the ends themselves are of doubtful value, the rewards not worth the effort needed to obtain them. If benefits come easily, well and good. If not, then work is necessary, but not so

136

important that it should dominate everything else. People whose life-style is based on that assumption are the despair of welfare workers and administrators. But perhaps they are not such non-conformists, after all. Their views, translated into slightly different terms, have a close counterpart among other Australians who favour increased leisure, freedom from responsibility, and a more relaxed attitude toward living.

In other words, while the practical expression of these views might appear to emphasize the contrast between them and all but a small section of the general population, the contrast is exaggerated. In the dilemma of 'mateship versus success', the one alternative is no more typically Australian than the other. Traditional Aboriginal culture and the phase of first contact aside, the patterns of adaptation have not departed too radically from the Australian-European subcultures around them. In pastoral areas, the range of models they could follow included 'bagmen' or 'swaggies', stockmen, and even overseers. In the cities there were the slum-dwellers with whom for the most part they lived side by side. Their place within the overall range was dictated by their economic circumstances and by special provisions and rules, and attitudes, which simultaneously helped and thwarted them. The aftermath of conquest, piecemeal and not marked by large-scale drama, became crystallized in squalid camps on the fringes of settlements or equally squalid houses in the poorer areas of the cities. And lacking the push-from-within which might have provided a means of escape through a combination of hard work and acquisitiveness, or a push-from-without through cleverly devised incentives, there most of them stayed.

No Aborigines today are living in a wholly traditional fashion free of outside influences. Even the very few who

137

have chosen to remain in the semi-arid spaces of the Western Desert, for example, have been affected—if only because the groups are so small that their customary arrangements are no longer workable. Nevertheless, an appreciable number of Aborigines in the North and parts of the Centre are still traditionally oriented—oriented toward their *own* traditions.

Two partly contradictory trends or moods are discernible here.

On the one hand are the pressures we have already outlined: the moves of government and other bodies in the direction of rapid and radical change. These are cumulative, and obvious.

On the other hand—and this in itself is an innovation of sorts—traditional Aboriginal culture has been accorded a positive place in the overall plan. It has, so to speak, become officially respectable. At the 1965 Conference of Commonwealth and State Ministers responsible for Aboriginal Welfare, the policy of assimilation was restated in a more flexible guise, spelling out the possibility of choice. The first part, therefore, now reads:

'The policy of assimilation seeks that all persons of Aboriginal descent will choose to attain a similar manner and standard of living to that of other Australians and live as members of a single Australian community—enjoying the same rights and privileges, accepting the same responsibilities and influenced by the same hopes and loyalties as other Australians . . .'

And the Commonwealth Minister for Territories, commenting on the revised wording, added: 'This change was made to avoid misunderstandings that had arisen that the assimilation policy sought the destruction of Aboriginal culture. It does not.'*

*'Further Steps in Aboriginal Assimilation', *Australian Territories*, Vol. 6, No. 2, April 1966, Canberra, pp. 34 and 35.

Anthropologists, and others too, have expressed concern at the ruthless disregard for Aboriginal traditions which marked the Australian scene from first contact until now. Policies and ideals might take those traditions into account, to a limited degree; but in practice, and with few exceptions, the outcome was always the same. People who opposed this one-way process were accused of wanting to keep the Aborigines as 'museum specimens', isolated in reserves instead of being allowed to mix freely with other Australians.

This, of course, would have been unrealistic. Given the trend of events, the traditional culture could not possibly have survived intact. Nevertheless, anthropologists pointed out, there was no reason why it should disappear altogether; more importantly, there was no reason why people of Aboriginal descent should be ashamed of that culture, as it was often suggested they should be. Their background was not the same as those of the 'newer' Australians who came later to this Continent; but, differences notwithstanding, it was a background of which they could, and should, be just as proud.

Official statements today accept this approach in principle. Aborigines in the north who have kept much of their traditional orientation, while becoming more articulate about their position in the wider context, make the same claim. Conscious of the changes in their own Aboriginal way—in religious ritual and ceremony, economy, marriage practices, social organization; in fact, in all its aspects—and accepting more and more of the 'new', they do not want to lose their own distinctive identity. Rather less expectedly, this point of view is gaining support in the south, among people only partly Aboriginal in descent with no personal experience of Aboriginal culture. They are influenced in this not by a simple nostalgia for the past, but by a feeling that they have been deprived of something of value. Recognizing that it is impossible to recover what they have lost, they are anxious not to lose all links with that background even though, for some of them, the ties are very slight indeed.

The seeds of separatism are here. Pressures toward assimilation, toward not only full acceptance but also absorption into the wider Australian society, are countered by these incipient pressures toward separate, 'Aboriginal', identity.

To most Australians, in the past, the balance between unity and diversity appeared to present few problems, at least in comparison with other countries where cleavages and differences were more apparent. With official policies stressing the ideal of relative homogeneity, the path has seemed clear. Nevertheless, in the perspective of the future, increasing attention will have to be paid, not only to the demands of immigrants from other countries seeking to keep something of their own past, but also to similar and perhaps more pressing demands from the First Australians. And in fact the greater liberality in official policy itself, whatever the reasons for that, has helped to make these demands more explicit and more articulate on the score of the continuing acknowledgment of Aboriginal identity.

Notes

1. Population.

One certainty, in 1973, was the continuing rise in the Aboriginal and part-Aboriginal population. Another was the unduly high infant mortality rate. But actual figures for the total Aboriginal population defined in *physical* (racial) terms are becoming less specific. Census counts cannot show the number of people who do not identify themselves as Aborigines — and whose 'Aboriginal' characteristics, if any, are so inconspicuous that they pass unnoticed by others. The two official categories now in use, probably mirror the current situation more accurately than a more ambitious attempt at breakdown could do: that is (i) more than 50% Aboriginal in descent (well over 46,000), and (ii) less than 50% Aboriginal (about 78,000-79,000). In short, and without noting some interesting cases of disputed affiliation, the trend is toward *social* identification and, particularly in (ii), a very large measure of personal choice; and in some reports the two are merged into one overall category, as 'Aboriginal'.

2. Census and Referendum, and Government.

In May 1967, the Australian public went to the polls to vote in a nation-wide referendum. It was in two parts. The first hinged on the numerical ratio between the House of Representatives and the Senate. The second dealt with Aborigines and contained two points wrapped into one question: 'Do you approve the proposed law for the alteration of the Constitution entitled — *An Act to alter the Constitution so as to omit certain words relating to the People of the Aboriginal Race in any State and so that Aboriginals are to be counted in reckoning the Population?*' To this, electors were asked to answer simply either 'Yes' or 'No'. The first part (omission of certain words) was designed to leave the way open for the Federal Government to legislate in relation to Aborigines. But the practical implications were not clear. Critics complained that this first part should not have been tied to

141

the second, neutral, point of formal census-taking — or that, at least, the Federal Government should have said more about its intentions. Many people read into this a concealed promise of Federal funds for Aboriginal welfare, but some of them contended that these could have been given anyway, without the threat of complete Federal control. However, spokesmen from all of the political parties supported the 'Yes' vote, which was, as the Press put it, 'Overwhelming'. Some months later, the Federal Government announced the formation of an Office of Aboriginal Affairs based in Canberra. A Minister for Social Services and Aboriginal Affairs (a dual portfolio) was appointed — the Hon. W. C. Wentworth, who had, in fact, been the driving force behind the establishment of the Australian Institute of Aboriginal Studies. An August 1968 Federal Budget announcement set aside $10,000,000 for Aboriginal welfare, approximately half of it for housing, education and health. Later, after a change in Prime Minister the Aboriginal portfolio was re-allocated.

In the 1972 Federal election, the Liberal-Country Party coalition was defeated and a Labor government came into power. Even before the first meeting of the new Parliament, the government was beginning to translate policy into practice. A new Department of Aboriginal Affairs was established. Federal Cabinet announced that nearly $11,000,000 would be spent on Aboriginal welfare during the current financial year, mainly on housing and special works projects, as 'a first step toward helping Aborigines'. Further sums were promised for other aspects of Aboriginal advancement, and new plans for wider Aboriginal participation.

The events of the 1960's and early 1970's are having cumulative effects, foreseen and unforeseen, on the socio-economic and political circumstances of people of Aboriginal descent. More than that, they have implications for the definition — the retrospective re-definition — of the content and meaning of traditional Aboriginal culture.

3. Chapter I: '... usually a minority to all intents ... inarticulate.'
This is still so. But the signs now point to a change. Today there are more Aboriginal spokesmen for people of Aboriginal descent, and their voices are much more likely to be heard. More Aboriginal committees and councils at State and Federal

142

levels are officially appointed or sponsored. And vigorous educational programmes should ensure that members of the next generation or so will be far more articulate — both as individual persons and, if they are so inclined, on behalf of the 'Aboriginal minority'.

4. Chapter I: 'Aborigine'.
Although the word 'Aborigine' is used fairly widely, we ourselves now prefer the alternative, 'Aboriginal' as the singular form, 'Aborigines' as the plural. A disadvantage of 'Aborigine' is that people tend to slip into the habit of using it as an adjective, or qualifier, as well as a noun — whereas 'Aboriginal', like 'individual', is now accepted as both.

5. Chapter II: '. . . their origin is shrouded in antiquity, and speculation is fruitless.'
Discussion continues on the score of Aboriginal 'origins', and the question remains open. But archaeological work now in progress may supply answers more solid than mere speculations. And genetic research is contributing obliquely, with a closer look at physical similarities and differences between the Aborigines and other peoples. They have been long enough on this Continent to develop their own distinctive genetic patterns — 30,000 years is now a conservative estimate. Not just for them, however, but for all the world's populations, the problem of 'who is like whom' has become enormously more complicated. Refinement in techniques and in categories of analysis has revealed cross-linkages and absence of linkages not suspected before, when the emphasis was on more obvious approaches through 'looking and measuring'. Physical appearance, especially, is only a rough-and-ready guide; and similarities and differences on that basis are defined in a very selective and arbitrary way.

6. Chapter II: 'Tribe'.
The word 'tribe' is useful, when we are looking at the Aboriginal situation in broad perspective. But it is important to remember that traditionally, for most purposes it was the smaller units that counted. (Apart from the various books which provide material on this topic, see R. M. Berndt, The Concept of 'The Tribe' in the Western Desert of Australia, *Oceania*, Vol. XXX, No. 2.)

7. Chapter VIII.

Some of these people mentioned here are now dead — Wonggu, for instance. Ngalmanagu, a widow, weak and lame, in her last years found even her quietest grandchildren too much for her. Mureimurei, even frailer, was a great-great-grandmother. Mauwulan (Mawulan) achieved fame as a bark painter, and with it a heightened interest in the commercial aspects of this new style of 'trading' with its wider orbit and its larger rewards. In a smaller way Midjaumidjau, no longer at Oenpelli, is now also a name for connoisseurs, working in the differing tradition of western Arnhem Land.

But this is not the place for detail, or for longer case histories. In singling out a few names from among so many, our aim was simply to underline the point that thinking and talking about Aborigines in a general way is not enough: that people reading about Aborigines for the first time need to keep in mind this equally important aspect of the Aborigines as *persons*. The 'romantics' who idealize them as invariably good and the hostile critics who disparage them as invariably bad — and both of these approaches are still current — are out of touch with reality. In any society there is a mixture of 'good' and 'bad', variously defined. And in any society, no matter what they hold in common, no two people are quite the same. The interplay between individual and society — between uniqueness and likeness, and between personal and group interests — is as relevant to the Aborigines as it is to *any* other situation where human beings are living together.

8. Chapter XI: The Jurawadbad (Yirawadbad) story.

Over the years we have been collecting more versions of this story — some from women, some from men. Its ritual associations have perhaps kept it from being partly or wholly forgotten, as so many others have been. (See R. M. and C. H. Berndt, *Man, Land and Myth in North Australia: the Gunwinggu People.* Ure Smith, Sydney, 1970.) But apart from Jurawadbad himself, the characters are not always named. In essence, the story remains the same — not only as told by the same people at different times, but also as between men and women; it is only that women's versions are invariably simpler, without the symbolic and ritual allusions that are central to those of fully initiated men.

144

9. Chapter XII: The *djunggawon* or *lorgan.*
The djunggawon is a ritual series from eastern Arnhem Land, the lorgan (or lorgun) from the west. They have a number of features in common. But the djunggawon is focused primarily on a stage of initiation, the circumcision of novices, whereas the lorgan is predominantly a mortuary sequence.

10. Chapter XIV: '. . . the art of a comparatively sophisticated people . . .'.
Here we are referring particularly to the north-eastern side of Arnhem Land, where contact with the outside world was of fairly long standing, and more consistent than in the west. But the art of western Arnhem Land could be described in these terms, too.

11. Chapter XVI: Rigidity.
Remember that this is a relative matter. Within each Aboriginal system the ideals, the normative patterns, were much narrower than the range of actual behaviour that was not only tolerated, but accepted. Nevertheless, the range of both ideal and actual was much more confined than in many other types of society. And emphasis on the past as the source of standards and guides to action in the present made for more than an appearance of conservatism. This emphasis did not preclude the existence of change and variation. But it did set certain limits to them, so that on the whole they were less obtrusive, and on a smaller scale, than in situations where innovation is accorded a more positive value.

Secret-sacred Matters.
Most traditionally oriented Aborigines in the past expressed no concern at the prospect of such matters becoming more widely known. It was their own local situation that interested them in this regard. For ourselves, we have always tried to ensure that material should not fall into the hands of people who were traditionally not permitted to see or to touch it. This is becoming much harder. It is not only that more such people, school children, for instance, and women, are literate, and have access to such material through means not open to them before. Also, it is because they are coming into contact with greater numbers of 'outsiders' who may, sometimes deliberately but perhaps more often without realizing the implications, bring it to their

attention. Even articles in obscure journals can be used in this way.

On the other hand, the attitudes of many Aborigines themselves are changing. A conservative core persists, but in certain regions even this is becoming more flexible. In eastern Arnhem Land, for instance, as one feature of the Elcho Island 'adjustment movement', objects formerly secret were put on public display. And both here and in western Arnhem Land women are making, for commercial sale, items, including bark paintings, once handled only by men.

There is no reason why some secrecy should not be retained where it is important to the people most directly involved: counterparts can be found not only in other religions, but also in the mundane or secular world. The glimpses we have included here and there do not in any way go contrary to that principle. They do not undermine the mystery, and the high significance, of Aboriginal religion. But that significance does not rest on secrecy; this is only one aspect, although it has received perhaps the greatest amount of attention. Aboriginal religion, in its various local manifestations, has a much more positive basis: and it can certainly take its place, if not among, alongside the 'great' religions of the world.

No outline of Aboriginal culture can be complete without more than a passing reference to the religion which was traditionally inseparable from it. Anything less would give a false picture, in a field where distortion (through over-romanticizing, the 'watering-down' of material thought to be obscure or unpalatable, or merely through misunderstanding or carelessness) is only too common. The Aborigines deserve better than this — not only in terms of physical welfare, but also in the image of themselves as presented, by themselves or by others, to their fellow Australians and to the outside world in general. Their religious beliefs and practices, although the special prerogative of people in certain areas, are of far more than local significance. And while this relates to the Australian population in general, it applies more specifically to that part of the Australian population which is Aboriginal in descent but not in culture. Pride in an Aboriginal past does not hinge on a revival of Aboriginal culture in the present; but an informed knowledge of that past does provide a more secure basis for a proper assessment of it as a background, not as a foreground, of action and aims in the future.

146

References

Berndt, C. H., 1950. *Women's Changing Ceremonies in Northern Australia.* Paris, L'Homme.

Berndt, C. H., 1961. The Quest for Identity: the case of the Australian Aborigines, *Oceania*, Vol. XXXII, No. 1.

Berndt, C. H., 1962. Mateship or Success: An Assimilation Dilemma, *Oceania*, Vol. XXXIII, No. 2.

Berndt, R. M., 1951. *Kunapipi.* Melbourne, Cheshire.

Berndt, R. M., 1952. *Djanggawul.* London, Routledge and Kegan Paul.

Berndt, R. M., 1959. The Concept of 'The Tribe' in the Western Desert of Australia, *Oceania*, Vol. XXX, No. 2.

Berndt, R. M., 1962. Tribal Marriage in a Changing Social Order, *Law Review*, Perth, Vol. V.

Berndt, R. M., 1962. *An Adjustment Movement in Arnhem Land.* Paris and The Hague, Mouton, Cahiers de L'Homme.

Berndt, R. M., 1964. The Gove Dispute: the question of Australian Aboriginal Land and the preservation of sacred sites, *Anthropological Forum*, Vol. 1, No. 2.

Berndt, R. M., 1965. Marriage and the Family in North-eastern Arnhem Land. In *Comparative Family Systems* (M. F. Nimkoff, ed.), Chapter 5. Boston, Houghton Mifflin.

Berndt, R. M. and C. H., 1951. *From Black to White in South Australia.* Melbourne, Cheshire.

Berndt, R. M. and C. H., 1954. *Arnhem Land, Its History and Its People.* Melbourne, Cheshire.

Berndt, R. M. and C. H., 1964. *The World of the First Australians.* Sydney, Ure Smith.

Berndt, R. M. (editor), 1964. *Australian Aboriginal Art.* Sydney, Ure Smith.

Berndt, R. M. and C. H. (editors), 1965. *Aboriginal Man in Australia.* Sydney, Angus and Robertson.

Capell, A., 1956. A New Approach to Australian Linguistics. *Oceania Linguistic Monographs*, No. 1. Sydney.

164

Douglas, W. H., 1958. An Introduction to the Western Desert Language. *Oceania Linguistic Monographs*, No. 4. Sydney.

Elkin, A. P., 1945. *Aboriginal Men of High Degree*. Sydney, Australasian Publishing Co.

Elkin, A. P., 1951. Reaction and Interaction: a food gathering people and European settlement in Australia, *American Anthropologist*, Vol. 53, No. 2.

Elkin, A. P., 1953/56. Arnhem Land Music, *Oceania*, Vol. XXIV, No. 2 to Vol. XXVI, No. 3.

Elkin, A. P., 1959. *Aborigines and Citizenship*. Sydney, Association for the Protection of Native Races.

Elkin, A. P., 1938/64. *The Australian Aborigines*. Sydney, Angus and Robertson.

Falkenberg, J., 1961. *Kin and Totem*. New York, Humanities Press.

Harney, W. E. and A. P. Elkin, 1949. *Songs of the Songmen*. Melbourne, Cheshire.

Hart, C. W. M. and A. R. Pilling, 1960. *The Tiwi of North Australia*. New York, Holt, Rinehart and Winston.

Hasluck, P., 1942. *Black Australians*. Melbourne, Melbourne University Press.

Hiatt, L. R., 1965. *Kinship and Conflict*. Canberra, Australian National University.

Kaberry, P., 1939. *Aboriginal Woman, Sacred and Profane*. London, Routledge.

Lommel, A., 1952. *Die Unambal, ein Stamm in Nordwest-Australien*. Hamburg, Monographien zur Völkerkunde.

McCarthy, F. D., 1938/58. *Australian Aboriginal Decorative Art*. Sydney, Australian Museum.

McCarthy, F. D., 1939. 'Trade' in Aboriginal Australia, and 'Trade' relationships with Torres Strait, New Guinea and Malaya, *Oceania*, Vol. IX, No. 4 to Vol. X, No. 2.

McCarthy, F. D., 1957. *Australia's Aborigines, Their Life and Culture*. Melbourne, Colorgravure Publications.

McCarthy, F. D., 1958. *Australian Aboriginal Rock Art*. Sydney, Australian Museum.

McConnel, U., 1957. *Myths of the Mungkan*. Melbourne, Melbourne University Press.

Meggitt, M., 1962/65. *Desert People*. Sydney, Angus and Robertson.

Mountford, C. P., 1948. *Brown Men and Red Sand*. Melbourne, Robertson and Mullens.

Mountford, C. P., 1948. *The Art of Albert Namatjira*. Melbourne, Bread and Cheese Club.

148

Mountford, C. P., 1958. *The Tiwi, their Art, Myth and Ceremony.* London, Phoenix House.

Mountford, C. P. (editor), 1960. *Records of the American-Australian Scientific Expedition to Arnhem Land*, Vol. 2. *Anthropology and Nutrition.* Melbourne, Melbourne University Press.

Mountford, C. P., 1965. *Ayers Rock. Its People, Their Beliefs and Their Art.* Sydney, Angus and Robertson.

Petri, H., 1954. *Sterbende Welt in Nordwest-Australien.* Braunschweig, Limbach.

Radcliffe-Brown, A. R., 1930/31. The Social Organization of Australian Tribes. *Oceania Monographs*, No. 1: or *Oceania*, Vol. 1, Nos. 1 to 4.

Reay, M. (editor), 1964. *Aborigines Now.* Sydney, Angus and Robertson.

Rose, F., 1960. *Classification of Kin, Age Structure and Marriage amongst the Groote Eylandt Aborigines.* East Berlin, Deutsche Akademie der Wissenschaften zu Berlin.

Sheils, H. (editor), 1963. *Australian Aboriginal Studies.* Melbourne, Oxford University Press.

Spencer, B., 1914. *Native Tribes of the Northern Territory of Australia.* London, Macmillan.

Spencer, B. and F. J. Gillen, 1904. *The Northern Tribes of Central Australia.* London, Macmillan.

Spencer, B. and F. J. Gillen, 1938. *The Native Tribes of Central Australia.* London, Macmillan.

Stanner, W. E .H., 1959-63. On Aboriginal Religion, *Oceania*, Vol. XXX, Nos. 2 and 4; Vol. XXXI, Nos., 2 and 4; Vol. XXXII, No. 2; Vol. XXXIII, No. 4; Vol. XXXIV, No. 1.

Strehlow, T. G. H., 1947. *Aranda Traditions.* Melbourne, Melbourne University Press.

Thomson, D. F., 1949. *Economic Structure and the Ceremonial Exchange Cycle in Arnhem Land.* Melbourne, Macmillan.

Tindale, N. B. and H. A. Lindsay, 1963. *Aboriginal Australians.* Brisbane, Jacaranda Press.

Turnbull, C., 1948. *Black War.* Melbourne, Cheshire.

Warner, W. L., 1937/58. *A Black Civilization.* New York, Harper.

149

Additional References

Berndt, C. H. and R. M., 1971. *The Barbarians.* (See Chapters 4 and 6.) London, Watts. (Penguin edition, 1973.)

Berndt, R. M., 1970. *The Sacred Site: the Western Arnhem Land Example.* Canberra, Australian Institute of Aboriginal Studies.

Berndt, R. M., 1973. *Australian Aboriginal Religion.* (In 4 Fascicles.) Leiden, Brill.

Berndt, R. M., ed. 1969. *Thinking About Australian Aboriginal Welfare.* Perth, University of Western Australia Press.

Berndt, R. M., ed. 1970. *Australian Aboriginal Anthropology.* Perth, University of Western Australia Press.

Berndt, R. M., ed. 1971. *A Question of Choice: an Australian Aboriginal Dilemma.* Perth, University of Western Australia Press.

Berndt, R. M. and C. H., 1970. *Man, Land and Myth in North Australia: the Gunwinggu People.* Sydney, Ure Smith.

Berndt, R. M. and E. S. Phillips, eds. 1973. *The Australian Aboriginal Heritage: an introduction through the arts.* Sydney, Ure Smith.

Bicchieri, M. G., ed. 1972. *Hunters and Gatherers Today.* (See Part 2 on Australia.) New York, Holt, Rinehart and Winston.

Crawford, I. M., 1968. *The Art of the Wandjina.* Melbourne, Oxford University Press.

Gould, R. A., 1969. *Yiwara.* New York, Scribner's.

Hunt, F. J., ed. 1972. *Socialisation in Australia.* (See Chapter 6.) Sydney, Angus and Robertson.

Hsu, F. L. K., ed. 1971. *Kinship and Culture.* (See Chapter 9.) Chicago, Aldine Publishing Co.

Lévi-Strauss, C., 1969. *Totemism.* Harmondsworth, Penguin.

Maddock, K., 1972. *The Australian Aborigines. A Portrait of their Society.* London, Allen Lane, the Penguin Press.

Mountford, C. P., 1968. *Winbaraku and the Myth of Jarapiri.* Adelaide, Rigby.

Mulvaney, D. J., 1969. *The Prehistory of Australia.* London, Thames and Hudson.

Mulvaney, D. J. and J. Golson, eds. 1971. *Aboriginal Man and Environment in Australia.* Canberra, Australian National University Press.

Pilling, A. R. and R. A. Waterman, eds. 1970. *Diprotodon to Detribalization.* East Lansing, Michigan State University Press.

Rowley, C. D., 1970-71. *Aboriginal Policy and Practice.* Vols. I-III. (The Destruction of Aboriginal Society; Outcasts in White Australia; The Remote Aborigines.) Canberra, Australian National University Press.

Stanner, W. E. H., 1968. *After the Dreaming.* The Boyer Lectures. Sydney, Australian Broadcasting Commission.

Strehlow, T. G. H., 1971. *Songs of Central Australia.* Sydney, Angus and Robertson.

Wallace, P. and N., 1968. *Children of the Desert.* Melbourne, Nelson.

The journals *Oceania* and *Mankind,* published in Sydney, both contain useful material on traditional as well as changing Aboriginal life. *Anthropological Forum,* published in Perth, has a broader coverage, but also has Aboriginal material. The Australian Institute of Aboriginal Studies (Canberra) is putting out a wide range of monographs on Aboriginal topics.

Acknowledgments

So many people have contributed, directly and indirectly, to the formation of this volume that it is quite impossible to list them, their works or their kindnesses. First and foremost, of course, are Aborigines. Our aim here is the same as it was when we prepared the first edition: we hope this book will help to increase understanding, appreciation and respect for a people who have had far less than their share of these in the past. More formally, we acknowledge our debt to Emeritus Professor A. P. Elkin, and the support of the Australian National Research Council (as it was then called), the Research Committee and the Department of Anthropology of the University of Sydney, the Research Grants Committee of the University of Western Australia, the Australian Research Grants Committee, and the Australian Institute of Aboriginal Studies.

In this reprinted edition, the number of photographs has been increased and some have been changed. All of the black and white illustrations which appeared in the original have been removed, except for six which appeared in the *Walkabout Pocketbook* edition. While we ourselves have a reasonably good colour coverage for some northern Australian regions, our Central Australian and Western Desert photographs are mainly in black and white. We are extremely grateful, therefore, to the friends and colleagues who kindly assisted us with colour. *Dr Bob Tonkinson* (of the University of Oregon) and *Mr Ian Dunlop* (of the Commonwealth Film Unit) have been most helpful. The scenes from the Western and Gibson Deserts represent virtually the last examples of people living in their natural environment with a minimum of outside contact. *Mr Noel M. Wallace* (Australian Institute of Aboriginal Studies) has provided a valuable series on Desert children and non-secret ceremony, obtained during the extensive fieldwork of himself and his wife. *Mr Charles P. Mountford* has, in fact, contributed the largest number. His collection is unique, especially since it covers material now comparatively rare. For northern areas, *Dr Maria Brandl* (Australian Institute of Aboriginal Studies) has supplied scenes of the well-known mortuary ritual from Bathurst and Melville Islands, and, her husband, *Mr Eric Brandl* (Northern Territory Administration), has supplied the outstanding examples of Aboriginal cave paintings.

152